METAVERSE INVESTING FOR BEGINNERS

A simple step-by-step guide to crypto art, digital assets in the

metaverse, crypto gaming and the future of the blockchain technology

Table of Contents

Introduction

Several offshoot branches of this notion have been developed over time, including the Metaverse, Metonymy, Meta politics, Metacommunity, and others. However, it has gained popularity, particularly among those in the cryptocurrency world. Every endeavor applies this particular title to itself to appear more fashionable than it is. I'm not sure what this is. This book will explain it in-depth and examine the possibilities of the Metaverse because it represents a huge paradigm change, and we are at the vanguard of it at this point. It's growing in importance, and I believe that it will be a common feature of your regular life over the next ten years. Now, let's break it down into words and go through it in depth so that, after reading this book, you will know precisely what the Metaverse is, without question in your mind.

Consider what it would be like to manage a business without a website. You are most likely to become obsolete in your field. In years to come, not having a presence in the Metaverse will render you as irrelevant as not having a website now. It will at the very least offer your competitors an advantage over you in the marketplace. Real and virtual worlds are becoming increasingly blurred, and their economies are becoming more entwined with one another. What occurs in one will impact the other; millionaires will be created, and businesses will go bankrupt as a result of their actions. A new digital large bank is being built, and a new digital universe is being created. This is the evolution of the internet.

Consider doing your company meetings and interviews in a virtual office rather than using zoom or webcam to communicate. If you can imagine putting on clothing while shopping from the comfort of your own home, you can imagine what the next big thing will be in teleportation technologies and Metanomics.

Imagine being able to attend work meetings from the comfort of your own home and having an experience that is even better than real life. This is possible because the Metaverse can provide an interface as seamless and straightforward as reality but with enhanced capabilities and capabilities.

Education has the potential to be intriguing as well. Imagine putting on those smart glasses and being able to peek into a human body, feeling a human heart and observing how organs communicate with one another. Atoms may be swiped in outer space and the cosmos expanded by your actions. It's going to be just incredible.

Among the most fundamental pieces of information concerning the Metaverse, as well as its relationship to your health, is included within this book.

Chapter One

The Metaverse

When the physical, augmented, and virtual worlds meet in a shared online arena, we call virtual reality. In a mirror world, also known as a virtual reality area, users may interact with a computer-generated environment and with other users in real-time. It's the Internet of the future, and it exists regardless of whether or not you are logged in to your account.

It's a permanent location where you may access change, live, and return. It will be available across all of our multiple computing platforms, including virtual reality (VR), augmented reality (AR), PC, mobile devices, and gaming consoles. In addition, the ecosystem considers users' needs, including an avatar, content production, a virtual economy, social acceptability, security and privacy, trust, and responsibility.

The Metaverse may be characterized as a multi-user real-time virtual realm in which individuals from all over the globe can connect via a network, co-exist, socialize, and trade value with one another. Compared to a standard multiplayer experience, the Metaverse distinguishes itself by the potential for users to create and exchange material that may be used to modify the environment around them in more or less persistent circumstances. For decades, World of Warcraft has operated in a virtual and digital Metaverse and a digital and virtual economy as part of a digital and virtual economy.

What is the purpose of the Metaverse, exactly? Because the Metaverse is the next frontier for online engagement, marketing and communication professionals must pay close attention to it, just as social media revolutionizes the online marketing environment. It opens up new options for business concepts previously restricted by our existing reality. Metaverse activities include video conferencing, cryptocurrency exchanges, email transmissions, virtual reality, social media postings and live streaming, artificial intelligence, blockchain technology, computer vision, and various other technologies. PeoAs a result, people engage with one another, play games, do commerce, and communicate with one another, among other things.

Individual innovators and artists will have tremendous potential due to the Metaverse. In addition, individuals who want to work and own homes in areas far from today's urban centers and people who live in areas where opportunities for education and recreation are more limited can benefit from this program. Finally, it is anticipated that individuals will be able to join the Metaverse wholly virtually through virtual reality, or interact with portions of their physical area through augmented and mixed reality, shortly.

Consider doing your company meetings and interviews in a virtual office rather than using zoom or webcam to communicate. If you can imagine putting on clothing while shopping from the comfort of your own home, you can imagine what the next big thing will be in teleportation technologies and Metanomics.

Metanomics

The suggestions above are excellent, but what can you do as a project manager, a business owner, or an individual to make a difference? Metanomics is the study of economic regulation and business models in the Metaverse, also known as the Metaverse. It is also investigating how real-world enterprises might incorporate virtual worlds into their overall strategy. If we go any further, Metanomics refers to the use of virtual worlds as laboratories to study real-world enterprises or public policy problems.

You may be now in a metaverse without even realizing it. Users often acquire digital items for the same reasons they do physical things: to save money. There is a sense of belonging and recognition to specific subgroups or communities, price speculation and the possibility of profit.

In the Metaverse, virtual fashion, avatar skins, virtual real estate, homes, and automobiles will be valuable assets. For example, recent automobile sales were hosted by the Netvrk, one of the most prominent crypto-metaverse initiatives, and the vehicles sold out in record time. With NFT's popularity showing no signs of waning, if you can create high-quality content and effectively market it, there are no limits to what you can accomplish in the Metaverse.

The Metonymy will consider the possibility of virtual careers. In addition to avatar designers, metaverse advisers, virtual real estate developers, automobile and property leasing, and hundreds of other job titles are available in the virtual world. Companies will have to change their marketing strategy from relying on online advice to surviving in a shared virtual economy to survive. Projects like envoy spring to mind as examples. Consider their decentralized board to be similar to an advertising board like Times Square in New York City.

Metanomics, according to some, is an asymmetric hedge against real-world occurrences. At the same time, according to others, Metonymy may one day become the purest form of capitalism, driven solely by free-market forces and driven wholly by the Meta-community. Additionally, the ease with which assets may be owned across borders may be pretty appealing to people who prefer to keep their money in a safe place.

Let's take it a step further. People will visit brands in the Metaverse because they have a solid emotional connection with them, rather than because they require a product or service. Therefore, while selling a product or service organically, you must provide your clients with the opportunity to lean into the experience.

As one example, Travis Scott performed for two weeks and earned $200,000 from clothing sales. Other artists have done the same. However, compared to the 1.7 million recordings he had in a single night for his in-person Astroworld tour and just under 40% of what he recorded from the 53.5 million times, this is a significant decrease in performance. Nevertheless, the ability to host events in virtual worlds for artists with a smaller fan base still exists, giving them the potential to promote digital record sales, enhance streaming traffic, and sell commemorative digital products.

Yes, the notion of a concert t-shirt from a decade ago may now be realized as an NFT or a game skin. Before this, you used to play games for fun and as a recreational activity; however, now is the time to make an investment and begin earning money.

The newer tech-savvy generation will move away from the existing antiquated education system and typical student occupations and instead earn a solid income from the Metaverse, which they will love. I will be brave enough to predict that this will happen. One guy stated that most employees can now be automated on the World Economic Forum. We would witness the development of a class of entirely worthless individuals. While one business sector closes its doors to the typical worker, another, more exciting sector with more prospects and possibilities opens its doors to AI and the web.

There are presently artificial intelligence social media influences. Artificial intelligence will now be used to enable, fill, and support the Metaverse's many functions. It may be possible to grow the Metaverse as the gaming industry's next frontier by using artificial intelligence (AI) tools that learn and understand the audience.

Another way artificial intelligence will play a role in the Metaverse is that AI systems will learn about you over time and tailor your metaverse experience to your preferences. For example, the founder of a virtual influencer agency depends on social listening and artificial intelligence to ensure that personas, speaking styles, and the audience they aim for are a perfect match. They may also modify and adjust the player's experience by presenting the most exciting material and interactions based on their specific characteristics.

Think of having a machine learning system that curates or even creates information and experiences explicitly suited to your needs, from constructing digital surroundings to moulding more realistic AI character behaviours to automating bug discovery. Artificial intelligence will have virtually endless possible uses in the future. As it pertains to the Metaverse and whatever eventual shape it may take, I believe artificial intelligence will be critical in bringing initiatives of this magnitude to completion.

Web 3.0 provides even greater capability and interoperability than any previously available services, including the Internet itself. The opportunities for remote employment, teleconferencing, telemedicine, remote socializing, and many other activities are greatly expanded. It is realistic to expect that the Metaverse will play an increasingly important role in the lives of ordinary people in the coming decade and beyond.

For example, metapolitics is just one of several subfields within this field. Social perspectives get a new dimension as a result of this development. The actual world may be influenced by social movements and trends, affecting the real world.

One day, we will require a single global blockchain, similar to how we currently have a single internet protocol upon which all websites and everything functions. But, unfortunately, interoperability and all of those various old currencies appear to be more of a source of friction and a hindrance to a seamless experience than anything.

Meta net is a term that has recently been coined. It has been in production for several years, and it is built on top of the original bitcoin system, which was developed in 2009. Today's date trades under the symbol BSV, which the cryptocurrency community has been socially engineered to despise.

I believe that a single global blockchain will be required. BSV is the only blockchain that, at this time, is capable of withstanding this degree of commercial demand or usage. According to Satoshi Nakamoto, the present Visa credit card network now conducts around 15 million Internet purchases each year throughout the world. Bitcoin already scales far more substantially than existing technology and at a fraction of the cost of the current hardware infrastructure. However, it never really reaches the upper limit of the scale. According to Moore's law, we may expect hardware speed to increase by tenfold in the next five years and by one hundredfold in the next ten years.

Even if Bitcoin continues to expand at its current acceptance rate, I believe that computer speeds will continue to outpace the number of transactions. For some reason, people are still striving to construct a speedier blockchain. According to Satoshi Nakamoto, the most influential blockchain produced so far is bitcoin in a private email to Mike Han on this information written around ten years ago.

A new version of the internet is now being developed, and it will have far-reaching repercussions for the rest of society. Marketing, communications, and branding professionals will confront new obstacles, but they will also have new possibilities to capitalize on the changing environment. Unique creativity will be unleashed in this new era of Metaverse, and new territories and horizons will be opened for brands and enterprises.

Individuals with entrepreneurial attitudes will benefit from this since it will open up new opportunities worldwide. The boundaries formerly established by one's background jurisdiction or educational level will be blurred to unprecedented degrees. Accept and make adjustments to the new paradigm that is emerging. In the same way that the internet and cryptocurrency were paradigm upheavals, the Metaverse combines that plus so much more. The question is, how are you preparing for this event?

Chapter Two

Blockchain and Cryptocurrency

Since Facebook changed its branding from social media to meta platforms, the Metaverse has risen to the top of the tech news agenda. The value of metaverse coins has skyrocketed in recent months, and this isn't a one-time occurrence. We've been on this metaverse path for years; it's only recently that Facebook's notable shift has brought this trend to the forefront of our attention.

Virtual commodities and nfts marketplace in augmented and mixed reality aren't all that the Metaverse has to offer. But that's only a sliver of the overall picture. It is the next step in the growth of the internet, and it will fundamentally alter our way of life, including the way we interact. This section will quickly examine where the trend is headed and, more significantly, how to enter this disruptive eight-trillion-dollar sector as a cryptocurrency investor and a stock market investor in the future.

It entails making investments in tokens that are particular to the Metaverse and tightly related to the creation and monetization of digital property. Also, don't forget about the cryptocurrency and blockchain technology that serves as the foundation for these metaverse ecosystems. Finally, we have several different actors in the stock market that are all heading in the same direction at the same time. So let's get this party started.

The Metaverse, if you haven't figured it out yet from my descriptions, is a virtual environment where individuals like you and me may participate in events such as concerts and conferences and vacations and holidays all over the world.

Imagine being able to customize a car you're interested in purchasing utilizing virtual reality and holograms in the next 10 to 20 years. Consider the possibility of using a projector to display your digital art on the wall of your actual dwelling. Art that you own in the form of one-of-a-kind NFTs is easily verified on the blockchain and very hard to steal. Contrary to popular belief, your home may burn down or be burglarized, but your digital assets are protected.

Imagine being able to attend work meetings from the comfort of your own home and having an experience that is even better than real life. This is possible because the Metaverse can provide an interface as seamless and straightforward as reality but with enhanced capabilities and capabilities. Slides can be advanced, links can be opened, and displays can be resized with a few swipes, taps, or pinches of the finger. Consider the possibility of seeing sports from any standpoint, possibly even from the athletes' perspective. Consider the case of remaining in touch with and experiencing feelings with your loved ones even when you are not physically present.

These are the kinds of things that future pioneers are thinking about and putting in place, and we're already halfway there. They've already had superfast broadband, speeds VR headsets, and constant always on 24/7 online worlds.

Many younger individuals aren't even aware that they need to transition to the Metaverse. However, as they get older, they have the assumption that a significant portion of their future will take place in the Metaverse. So, whether we like it or not, the rest of us will be forced to join the bandwagon.

On our path towards the Metaverse, what roles do blockchain and cryptocurrencies play in our lives? It turns out to be quite a lot after all. Several experts predict that today's cryptocurrency investors will be the Metaverse's rulers in the future. Why? This is because: Because video games are already well-established platforms, the transition into the Metaverse is expected to be a relatively straightforward process.

The decentralization enabled by blockchain technology allows people to regain control of their data while also encouraging innovation.

A vital component of the metaverse revolution is the creation of digital assets, which include cryptocurrencies and non-financial tokens (NFTs). You're looking at virtual assets that live on the blockchain and are managed by smart contracts, which you can read about here.

Who are the key participants in the cryptocurrency market in the Metaverse? Starting with the most established participants, the most significant market capitalizations are Axie, Decentraland, Sandbox, and Enjin. These are safe mid-cap cryptos with large market capitalizations.

Axie Infinity.

It is a game where you purchase, train, and breed animals that seem like pokemon but are nfts. Every single one of them is uniquely recorded on the Ethereum blockchain. You may trade and sell your axie on the marketplace for cryptocurrency, just as you would with any other nft.

Decentraland.

In a virtual environment built on the cryptocurrency ethereum, users may purchase and develop plots of virtual land, produce artwork, and do other activities. These assets are represented by one-of-a-kind nft tokens that can be traded on the marketplace. Have you ever had a go at playing the Sims or Second Life? If so, let us know about it. To be precise, you're looking at a blockchain-based replica of these classics.

Sandbox.

Now in a similar spirit to Decentraland, we've created the Sandbox. Players may create and profit from their game experiences in this virtual environment built on the ethereum blockchain. Its goal is to cause a rift between current game developers such as Minecraft and Roblox. Anyone may construct a game or fashionable design characters in the Sandbox and monetize these NFTs in the ethereum marketplace.

You have total control over your in-world creations in the decentralized world and the sandboxed world. There are no centralized platforms that limit what you can and cannot do. That is one of the advantages of blockchain technology.

Enjin coin.

This cryptocurrency is the grease that keeps the Enjin platform running smoothly. The Enjin platform is an all-in-one suite of tools that allows users to generate NFTs on the Ethereum blockchain and integrate them into games and other applications on the market. After you've looked into the well-known staples, you'll likely come across many promising new projects with favourable application scenarios.

For example, Effinity (EFI), a blockchain specialized in non-financial transactions developed by Enjin and built on Polkadot. There is more to say about Polkadot, and it will be addressed more as the discussion progresses.

OVR.

You have OVR, a digital layer covering the whole earth and has 1.6 trillion square kilometres of land. All of them are separate NFTs that you may purchase and sell. So they're effectively developing the first google earth on the blockchain.

Metahero

You may use their 3d scanner to create a digital representation of yourself. It is another 3d NFTs that can be utilized across gaming, VR, social media, and online fashion. For example, consider the possibility of using your 3D avatar to try on clothing that you might be interested in rapidly.

Is It Possible to Purchase These Metaverse Cryptocurrencies?

On the other hand, the more prominent mainstays may be purchased on any centralized exchange, such as Binance or Coinbase. They are also available for purchase within Defy. For example, the ethereum-based tokens may all be obtained through an old uni swap, but beware of the gas fees that will be charged. The traditional pancake swap method may get the binance smart chain tokens. So if you're ever in question, look up the token's market capitalization or coingecko.com and then click on the market tab. All the centralized and decentralized exchanges currently trading the coin will be listed.

To trade and stake in Binance, I have some of these coins listed on cryptocurrency exchanges. The lock staking pools on Binance make it simple to stake various coins, including sandbox, axie infinite, and a variety of other cryptocurrencies.

The number of people who utilize the Metaverse is increasing. Because the quality layer one and layer two stand to profit, investing in these blockchains may be the safer and smarter choice because you'll be diversifying your portfolio beyond the unique metaverse use cases. The cryptocurrencies listed here are ones that you can buy at a dollar-cost average over the years and retain for the long haul. If you purchase specific metaverse tokens, especially those with a lower market capitalization, you will need to monitor them more closely.

Polkadot is one of the layers to watch among these blockchains since it is all about interoperability and to link the many blockchains, which are primarily running in silos. That will become increasingly significant since you will be able to share your digital assets and NFTs across several blockchains in the future, as described above. So, for example, your ethereum-based NFTs don't need to be tied to the ethereum network. Furthermore, you do not require your Solana assets to remain on Solana and your cardinal assets to stay on Cardinal. This is why Polkadot's primary purpose is to facilitate interoperability. So that's something to be on the lookout for as well.

Blockchains and cryptocurrency are one method of constructing the Metaverse. Don't forget that all other firms, incredibly giant IT corporations, are working apart from the blockchain and contributing to its success. We're talking about a stock market worth a hundred trillion dollars. The meta-platforms come as an obvious choice here. In its previous incarnation, the digital behemoth was known as Facebook. It had already made considerable investments in virtual reality before its rebranding, including the acquisition of virtual reality firm Oculus in 2014. Following the Facebook rebranding project, Mark Zuckerberg is quite optimistic about the Metaverse. He believes he can completely replace the internet as we know it.

Microsoft

According to the company, Microsoft's Microsoft mesh platform is being used to create diverse and extended reality applications. It is a large-scale project that integrates the real world with virtual reality and holographic technologies. In addition, it is planned to include some of this technology into Microsoft teams for individuals who work from home. As a result, you will soon be able to incorporate mixed reality elements such as holograms and virtual avatars into your conference calls, which will be rather exciting.

Make sure to include equities that are related to infrastructure. For example, you've got hardware firms like Nvidia, the world's most powerful graphics and artificial intelligence chips manufacturer. In the crypto area, you've got Amazon, which has a cloud computing infrastructure that's frequently likened to the function that ethereum plays in the field. Many companies are established on Amazon web services, much as there are thousands of decentralized applications (Dapps) developed on the Ethereum blockchain.

All of these supporting firms are critical because, as the usage of the Metaverse grows, the need for computing power and data infrastructure will only grow. In addition, there is a slew of additional players involved in creating material for the Metaverse. For example, Epic Games, the firm behind Fortnite, whose CEO is quite optimistic about the Metaverse. They've already organized virtual concerts for artists like Ariana Grande and Travis Scott. In addition, they're working on creating photo-realistic digital people with their meta-human builder, which might allow you to design your digital doppelganger in future open-world games in the future. Although they are not currently a publicly-traded company, the epic games corporation is expected to attract a great deal of attention if and when they decide to go public in the future.

Unity Software.

In your possession is the Unity program, which produces the most extensively used engine in the whole video game business. In addition, the company claims they can assist in generating content for the Metaverse. This section will discuss Roblox, an online gaming platform that stores user-generated content and game scores at the end of this section. On the day that Roblox went public on the stock market, the company's CEO sent out a heartfelt thank you to everyone who has contributed to bringing the firm one step closer to realizing its goal of a Metaverse. In addition, several shoe companies and fashion houses, like Gucci, have partnered with them to provide mobile fitting rooms where you may try on garments and accessories for your virtual avatar.

If we look at the current situation, millions of individuals spend hours each day in virtual worlds and gaming platforms such as Roblox and Fortnite. This is a significant increase from previous years. In addition, over 2.7 billion individuals are categorized as gamers across the globe, translating into an industry worth more than 200 billion dollars each year, simply in gaming.

Virtual productivity platforms are rapidly expanding, particularly after the Covid 19 conference. Due to recent announcements from Facebook and Microsoft on new methods to work online, we now have hybrid offices, video-based schooling, and online social groups, to name a few of how we spend our time in digital places. In addition, we're seeing a rise in the use of non-financial assets and virtual assets. Nike has gotten in on the party with virtual footwear of its design.

As predicted by Bloomberg, the Metaverse would be an $800 billion business by the year 2024. Furthermore, Forbes estimates an eight-trillion-dollar total addressable market for the following social media generation, which is a huge opportunity. With its shift, Facebook has demonstrated that the Metaverse is not only an extension of the internet but instead its replacement.

Mark Zuckerberg wishes to be at the vanguard of this movement, but no one firm, to his knowledge, will be responsible for the creation of the Metaverse. A global technological action will be required to complete this voyage, which will take at least another ten years. The Metaverse will be a wholly integrated technological civilization with fire, electricity, the internet, and artificial intelligence. In the end, assimilation will occur, the opposition will be fruitless, and those who invest early in the process should be generously compensated.

Chapter Three

Stocks To Buy

The Metaverse is here, and it is the next step in the evolution of the internet. Since a result, it is possible that we may no longer be able to access digital information on our smartphones or laptops in the near future, as these devices may become obsolete. However, we will be completely immersed in a digital virtual environment and will be able to communicate with individuals all over the globe using smart glasses. Like it or not, the industry is coming, it's going to happen, and it will be worth $850 billion in the next seven to ten years, whether you like it or not. When it comes to enterprises, what are the stocks of companies that we may invest in in order to profit from the rise of the Metaverse? Let's have a look at this section to find out.

What is the Metaverse, and how does it work? The Metaverse can be defined in a variety of ways, but they all boil down to the same notion or concept. It has become the latest trending topic all across the world. The Metaverse is a shared virtual reality environment that we may enter using smart glasses and that is totally immersive. It is in this environment that our relationships will be multi-faceted. What is our current method of interacting with others? In social media, we communicate in two-dimensional or, at the most, three-dimensional environments, such as those found in some online games. However, thanks to the Metaverse, our interactions will be multi-dimensional 4D, allowing people to immerse themselves in digital information rather of merely watching it, rather than simply viewing it.

For example, imagine yourself in the future participating in a zoom conference where you can see people's faces online and you're in a virtual environment with an avatar meeting people from all over the world in whatever beautiful dream place you want. Another example would be playing chess with someone on the other side of the planet with the use of a virtual reality environment. So, if you recall the movie-ready player1, it's exactly the same as it was before.

It is possible to dance with someone halfway around the world when you put on virtual reality glasses in a virtual environment. To a greater extent, you might go surfing in the desert or wherever else, much as in the movie Matrix. The Metaverse is going to fundamentally alter the way we work, play, and learn in the future. I'm not sure how you feel about it, but I find it to be rather intriguing and unusual. For instance, how would you like to work in the future? The applications will no longer be accessible through a laptop or tablet; instead, you will put on the glasses, and the programs will appear everywhere around you.

Do you remember the Tom Cruise program Minority Report, where he was always swiping things and extending them, or even how Tony Stark did it in Iron Man, when you had to move things about with the hologram? What will happen in the Metaverse is exactly what I predicted. Our applications will be everywhere around us, and we will be able to drag and drop files into and out of our virtual area. Consider the possibility of future encounters in which we will be able to meet with individuals all around the world using avatars in whatever venue we want.

If you think about it, all of this progress might mean that things like zoom, smartphones, and tablets become outdated in the near future, and you will not be surprised. Consider the possibility that corporations like as Apple or Samsung will not pivot to this Metaverse in the future. Because technology is evolving at such a rapid pace, their products may become as obsolete as video cassettes were in the past.

What's equally intriguing is how the Metaverse might alter the way in which we interact with video games. Watching the Facebook Video, where it dubbed itself as meta, you would be able to fence with someone from another nation just by putting on a pair of virtual reality glasses. You see their avatar, they see you, and you begin to fence with each other.

Education has the potential to be intriguing as well. Imagine putting on those smart glasses and being able to peek into a human body, feeling a human heart and observing how organs communicate with one another. In outer space, atoms may be swiped and the cosmos expanded by your actions. It's going to be just incredible.

Another industry with an estimated value of over one trillion dollars by 2028 has been identified. Interestingly, some of the most well-known businesses in the world are taking this seriously and are already establishing a presence in the Metaverse in their own manner. So, for example, Nike is secretly preparing for the Metaverse by developing new products. They have filed seven trademark applications in order to sell virtual sneakers and apparel in the Metaverse that are branded with their logos.

Again, we will have an avatar in the future Metaverse and will be able to communicate with individuals all over the world. To make your avatar appear more appealing, you may purchase Nike sneakers, clothing, and sweatshirts for your avatar. Nike will offer them to you in the virtual world, according to the company. They are now making all of these virtual Nike items, and not only for Nike, but also for Gucci and other luxury brands.

Gucci has lately released digital accessories, clothing, and bags, which are available for purchase on the Roblox gaming platform. What exactly is Roblox? Roblox is a virtual world that is quite similar to the metaverse. It is an online game environment. People are already interacting with one another in this online game environment, purchasing Gucci clothing, swapping them, and doing virtual retail transactions. They recently opened a Gucci garden space on Roblox, which you can check out here. It is possible that some people were able to resale these Gucci products, including Gucci glasses, Gucci bags, and Gucci clothing, for as little as one dollar to as much as nine dollars on the internet. They purchased it for four dollars and seventy-five cents, and they then sold this Gucci bag, which was a virtual digital bag, on the Roblox site for $4000. There will be millions to be made in the Metaverse, just as there will be millions to be made in the actual world. For brands and businesses to take this seriously today is because they have realized that it is no more a passing trend or figment of their imagination. It's actually occurring. Entering the Metaverse will become a need for brands in order to remain relevant in the future. How much of a company's shares will be required for the creation, construction, and maintenance of the Metaverse, as well as for the company's profit from the next development of the internet? Hundreds of stocks will gain from the Metaverse, but I will concentrate on the most important ones and separate them into metaverse stocks that are absolutely necessary.

The Corporations.

The first group would include businesses that are involved in the development of hardware, operating systems, and metaverse software. These are firms who are developing smart glasses and taking them to the next level, and they are also in the process of developing the operating system that will power the Metaverse's virtual reality environment. We will also include firms that are involved in the construction and maintenance of the Metaverse's infrastructure, which will be accomplished using cloud computing. There are several firms, but the ones I'm going to concentrate on are as follows:

Meta

Assuming you haven't been living under a rock, you're probably aware that Facebook has renamed itself as Meta. As a result, their ticker symbol, FB, will be changed to MVRS on December 1st, 2018. What is the reason behind Facebook's meta-branding? To be the dominant player in the Metaverse is their long-term strategic goal, according to their mission statement. Because they control the Oculus VR headsets, games, and the virtual reality headgear, they have a significant technological advantage over the rest of the competitors in terms of hardware and software.

Their collaboration with Ray-ban has resulted in the development of ray-ban tales, the company's latest iteration of smart glasses. They are the ones who are at the head of the pack. Microsoft is now a close second, and the two companies are working together on Meta.

Microsoft

Microsoft's CEO has also stated that the company will develop the enterprise component of the Metaverse. That is where they envision professionals meeting, collaborating, and working together in the future, all within a virtual world populated by avatars, as they do now. Microsoft has also made an investment in their own smart glasses, the Hololens.

Amazon

Amazon has also revealed its plans to enter the Metaverse, where they would establish a virtual economy and virtual stores that users will be able to visit while in the virtual economy. For example, if you want to buy a shirt, you may use Virtual Tryons to make sure it fits well. Cloud computing services are required for the construction and maintenance of the Metaverse's infrastructure. Amazon web services by Amazon and Microsoft Azure are the two most powerful companies in the market. In addition, there are alphabet online services available. All of these would be essential in the construction and maintenance of the metaverse infrastructure.

The tools that are used in the development of content.

The Metaverse cannot be developed by a single corporation or by a single individual. Millions of computer programmers, designers, and developers from all around the globe will work together to construct it. It will be a collaborative effort on a worldwide scale, similar to Wikipedia. As a result, in order for all of these people to develop material for the Metaverse, such as virtual real estate, virtual buildings, and virtual avatars, they will require tools to do so. In order to develop these metaverse settings, what are the names of the firms that give the tools? The first is the ticker sign ADSK, which stands for Autodesk.

Autodesk

Autodesk is the world's leading provider of software for architects, engineers, and those working in the construction industry. Before a builder begins work on a physical structure, he or she uses 3D modeling software known as AutoCAD to develop the blueprints. Recently, Autodesk released a set of tools that enable computer programmers to design VR and AR 3D structures and simulations, such as virtual reality and augmented reality buildings and infrastructure, using 3D modeling software.

It goes without saying that Autodesk would be a vital software tool for anyone who wish to develop metaverse settings. We will return to the ADSK stock in a few days to further examine it. The ticker symbol RBLX for the Roblox company would be the next stock to investigate.

Roblox

Roblox is an online gaming platform with a current monthly active user base of 164 million people. You could use Roblox to create your own game if you wanted to. In addition, you may build your own games and participate in those produced by other people. These games are similar to a metaverse game in which you play as an avatar and interact with other players. You may use them to sell items and purchase goods from other people, and there is a local Roblox money that functions similarly to a virtual economy within the site.

The Roblox platform, much like the Gucci bag that can be purchased digitally within the Roblox virtual environment, will be an essential tool for those who wish to build games in the Metaverse, just as the Gucci bag is in the real world. The next stock to be discussed is the Unity software ticker denoted by the letter U.

Unity Software

The Unity software will also be a critical tool for programmers who will be creating metaverse games in the future. As the foremost 3D video game engine designers, they are responsible for customizing the way in which video game players move and interact with their games. Unity engine is used by 94 out of every 100 game production firms. Unity would be a key role in assisting firms in the creation of distinctive metaverse presences and surroundings. They have professional software and gaming services tools at their disposal. In addition to these firms, there are others such as Tech Two Interactive, Electronic Arts, Metapod, and others. There are a few additional stocks to consider, but these are the most important.

Semiconductors are a kind of semiconductor.

Because semiconductors are the fundamental building elements of any digital economy, it is impossible to avoid dealing with them. To keep the Metaverse running, you'll need a lot of semiconductors. There are a plethora of semiconductor stocks available today. The first group would include semiconductor businesses that specialize in the design of high-end chips.

Nvidia

Nvidia is the market leader, and you also have AMD on your side. In addition to Nvidia, there are a few others, but Nvidia would be the most prominent in terms of high-end processor design. Nvidia is exclusively responsible for the design of the chips. They are not the ones who create the chips. So, who is responsible for the production of these high-end chips? Well, Taiwan Semiconductor Manufacturing Company, ticker symbol TSMC, is responsible for manufacturing 90 percent of these high-end sophisticated chips with a size of less than five nanometers.

Although there are other semiconductor businesses that are closely connected to Nvidia and TSMC such as ASML, Applied Materials, Alarm Research, and many more, Nvidia and TSMC would be the two major candidates.

These are the few important stocks to own if you want to profit from the emergence of the Metaverse in the near future. By the way, if you're looking to invest in an ETF, there's also a metaverse ETF that you can purchase. The metaverse ETF has the thickest symbol, which is Meta, and it's the most expensive.

Discover the secrets to being a successful stock investor.

Being a successful investor requires more than simply understanding what to buy. You may already know what you want to buy, but that isn't enough. When it comes to becoming a great investor, there are four things to look out for. They are as follows:

- You must be aware of what you are purchasing.

- You must be aware of the best time to purchase the stock. You must be aware of the number of shares you should purchase.

- You must know when to sell and when to collect your earnings.

Many people have the problem of knowing what they want to buy but purchasing it at the incorrect moment. They purchase when a stock is overvalued, overpriced, or overextended, among other things. Consequently, simply understanding what to buy is not enough; you must also understand when to acquire it. As an example, when it comes to investing, you only need to acquire shares in these firms when they are significantly cheap in the market.

For example, Meta, or Facebook, is presently undervalued, and Nvidia is currently overpriced, yet TSMC, with ticker symbol TSM, which is a Taiwan semiconductor manufacturing company, is somewhat undervalued at the present. So you need to know which stocks are discounted and which ones are overvalued, because if you buy a good stock that is expensive, you might end up losing money.

How would you determine the genuine worth of a company and how would you compute its intrinsic value? When a stock is undervalued and prices have retraced to a support level on the chart, it is a good time to buy. When it comes to timing your entrance, you must consult the technical charts. It all comes down to how well you time your entries. The firm is a fantastic one, but it is expensive, and the stock is now overextended in terms of price. Ideally, the price would retrace closer to a support level before you began constructing a trade.

Consider the fact that Meta or Facebook is underappreciated and is now at a support level when creating this book. Some of them are available for purchase right away, while others would be better suited for holding off till they become more appealing.

Also keep in mind that there are certain equities in which you do not need to invest but in which you might trade for a limited period of time. Companies that are currently profitable and generating cash flow are the only ones I like to invest in in order to evaluate their intrinsic worth. However, some stocks are not making money and are still losing a significant amount of money, so I would not recommend investing in them, but they have the potential to rise in value.

These are stocks that are intended for short-term trading. If you are going to trade, you should know where to position your stop loss and profit objective, as well as how to join and exit trades with the most possible gains and the least amount of risk. Furthermore, how can you use options to reduce your risk while increasing your reward? As an example, be cautious because both Roblox and Unity are not producing any money at the time of publishing this information. They are still incurring losses, and their stock is significantly overvalued. While you shouldn't invest in these equities, you should consider utilizing options to make a short-term swing trade on these stocks. Learn more about investing in and trading in these metaverse stocks, as well as other outstanding equities available on the black market, by visiting our website.

Chapter Four

Investing in the Metaverse

It is possible that investing in the Metaverse will prove to be one of the most spectacular possibilities for knowledgeable investors to make a tremendous amount of money in the future. Following Facebook's recent rebranding to meta in order to further develop their vision and interpretation of the Metaverse, the company has piqued the interest of investors around the world in terms of how they can potentially invest early in this space and profit from what could be a fantastic investment opportunity.

Indeed, there are a variety of interesting and diverse methods to invest in the Metaverse, which extends beyond traditional stock market investments. As the Metaverse gets more and more integrated into our daily lives, it becomes something in which we are more interested. It undoubtedly exists in what could be considered a more virtual environment, and I anticipate that the investment opportunities associated with it will only grow in scope over the course of time. In this section, we'll go over the early investment opportunities that are available.

Stocks

The very first investment possibility that I wanted to talk about is investing in stocks. Most investment portfolios, including mine, rely on it for their primary source of income. In addition, there are a plethora of different firms that are actively contributing to the Metaverse and the infrastructure that is necessary for the development of the metaverse ecosystem.

Our knowledge base already has information on Mark Zuckerberg's plans to develop his own Metaverse and stake his claim on the evolution of social networking in the future. In this particular case, however, it's worth noting that the Metaverse in itself extends much beyond the capabilities of a single corporation, because the infrastructure required to construct a metaverse, as well as the activities that will take place within it, are significantly more extensive.

It encompasses everything from gaming with friends in a virtual world to attending live events and entertainment, getting personal training without having to go to a gym, working with colleagues and holding meetings in a virtual office, and even going shopping in the Metaverse, among other activities. Imagine all the many enterprises currently running, establishing, and having a physical product they could turn into a digital or virtual product and put into the Metaverse.

Unity software and Roblox are examples of gaming firms. Peloton is an example of a fitness company. Video conferencing companies such as Zoom and Microsoft are examples of e-commerce companies such as Amazon and Shopify. All of the businesses mentioned above have a plethora of opportunities. As a result, there are numerous opportunities to invest in and gain exposure to some of these stocks as part of your overall investment portfolio strategy. Inevitably, it will be fascinating to see which stocks decide to make a move and begin investing in the company in order to obtain some exposure into the Metaverse and aggressively seek to gain some market share. I anticipate that the first-mover advantage in this sector will be significant.

For the Metaverse, the market potential, or the predicted market opportunity, is expected to be 825 billion dollars by 2028, and to rise at a compounded annual growth rate of 43.3 percent per year. The Metaverse offers a plethora of investment prospects for organizations that may benefit from massive amounts of development in their business simply by investing in it and offering some type of virtual product within it.

Token for use in the metaverse.

Following that, there are a couple additional investment ideas that are a little bit more attractive. As a result, we're going to start by talking about metaverse tokens to begin with. A website like coinmarketcap.com, for example, allows you to navigate over and click on the metaverse page, which displays some of the most popular metaverse cryptocurrency coins.

We have tokens like as Axie Infinity, Decentraland, Enjin currency, and the Sandbox, amongst others. All of this has variable market capitalizations, particularly with axie infinite and Decentraland, which have market capitalizations ranging from close to six billion dollars to over nine billion dollars. These aren't some insignificant trinkets. They are digital tokens in which a large number of individuals are actively investing. These tokens are essentially the same type of currency that would be used in the matching virtual metaverses that they have created for you to explore.

I suppose you might draw a connection to spending a lot of money in England to buy items, for example. The same may be said for these virtual or metaverses, as they are sometimes referred as. For example, the AXS token is associated with Axie Infinity, the MANA token is associated with Decentraland, and the SAN token is associated with Sandbox.

These tokens are attracting the attention of investors. Because they feel that their corresponding Metaverse may be the next great thing, they're utilizing the tokens to purchase items within that Metaverse and are looking to invest in this token as a pure investment opportunity. That said, it's amazing to see how much the value of these metaverse tokens has increased since Facebook announced its rebranding. The price of the Decentraland token increased by 75 percent in a year, reaching its market top of $3.56. As of today's market pricing, the token is still trading at roughly $3.17 per token, which is a relatively low price compared to other cryptocurrencies like bitcoin. Our growth rate has increased by 300 to 400 percent in the last three weeks, which is unprecedented.

In essence, by investing in these metaverse tokens, you are putting your faith in the popularity of the associated Metaverse to rise over the course of time. Because of the increase in demand, you will be able to purchase more items within the Metaverse, causing the price to rise over time.

When it comes to investing in some of these metaverse tokens, there is a certain amount of subjectivity involved. Decentraland has a current market capitalization of six billion dollars, but what actually qualifies as a billion dollars?

Ultimately, it all boils down to supply and demand, as well as prospective competitors within the market. Some of these tokens, however, remain impossible to assign an underlying worth to because of their complex nature. I believe that the upside potential for some of these crypto-built metaverses, especially with the anticipated rise of these metaverses, may be incredibly enormous.

Land and property are two terms that come to mind.

My use of the terms "land and property" does not refer to land and property in the traditional sense. I'm referring to land and property in some of the metaverses that are currently under construction. Within these metaverses, you could really purchase pixels that represented land and ownership rights.

We are all aware of the wonderful investment Disney made a few decades ago when he purchased 27000 acres of property in Orlando, Florida, for about $182 an acre, a bargain at the time. Today, the land itself is worth several billion dollars, and it looks that the same type of potential possibility exists in the Metaverse. You'd be amazed at how much money some of this land is presently selling for, if you knew how much it was worth. If we want to purchase some land in the sandbox metaverse, we may do so by clicking on the buy land button. This will then take us to a page where many individuals can purchase NFTs and other types of digital assets. You can see how pricey some of these areas are just looking at them. It's just a ridiculous situation.

In the recently sold section, you can see that legal land is selling for anywhere between 1.5 and 2 ethereum, depending on the theme of the property. That is most likely worth around $4500 at the moment on the market. This price of land has the potential to rise to about nine thousand dollars simply for a few pixels on a computer screen. Then, when you've gone ahead and purchased the property, it displays on the metaverse map, where you can see a variety of different symbols representing individuals who have purchased land inside the company.

Atari is clearly visible in the shot above. Another video game business appears to have purchased property in the sandbox metaverse, this time for the purpose of developing games. Individuals and potential businesses that have purchased land in the sandbox metaverse may be found in their hundreds across the metaverse.

You could wonder how investing in this land and purchasing land within these metaverses is a type of financial opportunity, and I can understand your confusion. As I previously stated, as the number of individuals who utilize this Metaverse and its tokens grows, the amount of land available for purchase becomes increasingly limited since so many people have already purchased it. The notion of supply and demand is effectively established at this point. Due to a restricted supply, people can demand whatever price they believe they will be able to sell their property for.

What's fascinating is that you may continue to build on the landing that you've already established.. If you were to sell the land at a later date, you might demand a higher price for it since it would be more appealing to people if it had more infrastructure. If you consider yourself to be a fairly clever landowner and investor in some of these metaverses, you should have a look at some of the markets available on many of these different metaverses to see what you can find.

NFTs and Wearables

Non-fungible tokens are things that people have argued have no value at all in the real world, but which have the potential to have significant value if used and applied in the virtual world. This is especially true if you are transitioning as a human species from placing greater value on your physical assets and items to placing greater value on your digital assets and items in which you are a part of, such as cryptocurrency. The possibility exists that you will be the only owner of an NFT, which you may place in your virtual property to sit on the virtual land in your Metaverse where people are presently flexing in their fancy clothing and luxury automobiles. With NFTs and wearables, you might possibly witness the same type of thing in the Metaverse as you would in the real world. It's an intriguing thought, and it's one that's surely a little bit mind-blowing simply to think about it for a moment.

Market Development Opportunities in the Metaverse

The majority of the time, I believe that these metaverses will be used by a bunch of 12-year-olds who would run around with their avatars in the virtual worlds, but the reality is quite different from my expectations. The amount of money that is spent on these platforms is truly huge, and it is simply mind-boggling to contemplate the scale of it.

Consider the following example: on axie affinity, the most expensive item ever sold was 300 ethereum, which at today's market price would be around 1.35 million dollars or the equivalent of almost a million pounds sterling. The amount of money that is being spent on some of these digital assets is ridiculous. The NFT space has seen it, and now we're starting to see it over in these metaverses as well, which is exciting. In my opinion, this is a potentially enormous investment opportunity if you know what you're doing and which assets are the most appropriate ones to invest in since some of them are unquestionably really valuable. On a related topic, you may find something known as wearables in these virtual worlds as well.

Consider the following scenario: you have an avatar in a virtual environment. You will need to dress up the avatar with various accessories and one-of-a-kind goods that are only available to that avatar in order to complete the look. Take, for example, one of the markets in the Metaverse to demonstrate what I mean.

In the Decentraland marketplace, you may find a wide variety of NFT, wearables, and collectibles that you can actively use to customize your avatar's appearance.

You can see the various pricing for the various variables, ranging from 70 tokens to 1500 tokens and even down to five tokens in certain cases. The value of these various digital assets is largely determined by the degree to which they are rare in the first place. So you've progressed from common assets that you can purchase all the way up to unique assets that are one-of-a-kind collections, such as the one below, which is an ethereum dusk ghost helmet priced at 2500 tokens, which is roughly equivalent to approximately seven and a half thousand dollars in real currency.

It's one of those things that depends on supply and demand, especially if the item you're purchasing is a little out of the ordinary. When more people begin to use the Metaverse, the price of those rare items will rise in value as demand increases and more people begin to use these metaverses. Because rare items are in limited supply, the price of those items will rise in value as demand increases and more people begin to use these metaverses. These are just a few of the several ways in which you might make an investment in the future of some of these metaverses.

Chapter Five

The Truth About Investing in The Metaverse

In the end, the sad reality is that metaverse investments are not a suitable fit for the vast majority of investors. I'd want to share some of my experiences with you on investing in the Metaverse. Listed here are the lessons I've learnt over the previous five years, as well as what I hope to achieve by 2022. I'd want to share some insights or suggestions with you about how to take advantage of the next technology change.

First, how about taking a different perspective on the Metaverse? It is the merging of the physical and digital worlds that is referred to as the Metaverse. It consists of augmented, mixed, and virtual reality experiences. There's a lot more to it than that, but the Metaverse is the next evolution of mobile internet. This iteration isn't about fitting more information onto a smaller computer, but rather about creating a fully linked and immersive environment or universe.

Adobe has provided an excellent illustration of how smoothly the Metaverse may replace the applications we presently use on our phones and desktops. The Metaverse encompasses much more than just entertainment. It encompasses the places where we work, where we practice medicine, and the places where we cooperate with others. It is throughout our schooling that we learn logistical skills such as navigation and how to do practical day-to-day duties. Their upcoming AR site, platform, and authoring system will let users to produce all of the processes, DIYs, and checklists that they use on a daily basis in a metaverse-native format, and they will be available for download in the near future. Some of them are quite technical, such as mending a fuel line on a fighter plane, while others are more mundane, such as baking the ideal banana bread. Even if this technology is implemented effectively, it is not something that you would be aware of while it is in place. It's an intuitive form of technology that operates in the background, and there are several options available right now.

Venture Capital - A type of financing that is used to fund new ventures.

Since 2005, I have spoken with hundreds of venture capitalists, angel investors, and partners at private equity firms. I have also invested my own money in the companies I have spoken about. In fact, I'm aware that a number of you are members of the investor community who are interested in investing in metaverse firms.

The unpleasant reality is that metaverse investments are not a suitable fit for the majority of investors. The technology of the metaverse is rather specialized, and the business is still in its infancy; we're talking about the internet in 1996 here. The majority of investors who I talk with want to see a normal return or a ROI within five years or less. Those unfamiliar with the startup world may not realize that when an investor provides startup capital in exchange for stock or partial ownership in the firm, the investor anticipates that the startup will be purchased or go public within five years of receiving the funds. Companies are issuing initial public offerings (IPOs) every five years, if at all. They anticipate that you will be acquired or purchased within five years. That is simply not a realistic expectation for the majority of metaverse businesses today. Investors must be prepared to play for the long haul, and not every investor is capable of doing so. To further complicate matters, the firms that will bring the most value to the Metaverse and go on to become the next unicorns or those who will be developing behind-the-scenes goods will be the ones that do so.

Because these goods are not always simple to comprehend, the combination of having a long return on investment term and investing in hot startups makes it tough to visualize products and makes the link between venture capital and the Metaverse difficult to explain. It is only appropriate for a specific type of investor.

Traditional technologies are being replaced by the metaverse.

Consider the ways in which the Metaverse is displacing conventional technological systems. It will assist in providing some perspective for the market potential that we will be discussing later.

I believe that many people, especially investors, believe that augmented and virtual reality will entirely replace present modes of communication overnight. It is possible that phones could be turned off and everyone will be wearing a headset, although this has not happened in the past.

At initially, new technology is complementary to existing forms, but with time, it gradually replaces those forms. We were able to hear it because of the audio. For a long time, radio broadcasts could only be heard on a real radio, but quite early in the history of the internet, people were able to listen to radio broadcasts online. It was still the same radio show that could be heard on AM or FM radio stations; it was simply made available on the internet as a new means for people to listen to it.

Then, as time went on, we began to get radio programmes that were only available on the internet. This evolved into podcasts, and now we have an entire generation of people who only consume long-form audio content through podcasts, as opposed to other means. A significant shift has occurred, and it has occurred in phases. It wasn't something that happened overnight.

Another recent example is the Travis Scott concert in Fortnite, as well as the mini Nas x concert in Roblox, all of which are now available. These musicians are not intended to take the place of conventional concerts. They're just including these as a means of connecting with their followers and providing a means for their fans to consume their music. Many of the habits we have now will gradually be replaced by virtual ones as technology advances. As previously said, it is not a complete paradigm change, but rather a series of little, progressive movements.

Market opportunity.

We've reached the most thrilling section of the story. Approximately 800 billion USD will be available in the Metaverse market by 2024, according to a report by Bloomberg. See the value and potential that exists inside the Metaverse.

What is the best way to invest?

Here's what I'm keeping an eye out for in 2022, which is divided into three categories: indexes, stocks, and the passage of time. Index funds are the first that come to mind, and so far, I've only come across one index fund that specifically targets entities in the metaverse, a round hill ball metaverse exchange-traded fund or ETF.

ETF

The round hill ball metaverse index is the first index created specifically to measure the performance of the Metaverse and is available to everyone in the world. Nvidia, Roblox, Cloudflare, snap (which owns Snapchat), Facebook, and AutoDesk are among the firms included in the portfolio, which is weighted according to a tiered system. All of them are actively engaged in the construction of the Metaverse. There's a lot more, but that's only a handful of them. You can find this ETF by searching for it in the meta section of your preferred brokerage and reading about it.

Stocks.

There are several particular public firms in the Metaverse in which you may invest in shares, as well as a leading player from the standpoint of the platform. You should keep an eye out for publicly traded firms such as Unity Technologies, Nvidia, Qualcomm, Broadcom, and any wireless tower companies such as Verizon.

There are end-user platforms that operate behind the scenes, as well as architectural businesses that offer all of the support necessary to keep the metaverse running. That is the area with the greatest potential for growth. This category, in my opinion, also includes content companies, which I thought some of you might be interested in learning more about. Personally, I'll be watching to see how streaming services such as Netflix, Hulu, Disney, and Amazon react to the creation of content in virtual and augmented reality environments. I'm simply going to seek for those that are doing it very well. I said before that a virtual Travis Scott performance last year generated $20 million in revenue for the music promoter. It's a very good bet that consumers will pay for other sorts of media in immersive environments as well, based on the chances.

Neither of the two groups I described are concerned with private enterprises or startups; instead, they are concerned with publicly listed corporations. Unless you are a member of the venture capital (VC) community, you will not have the opportunity to invest in these firms. A few possibilities, such as republic start engine and a number of other crowdsourced venture capital platforms, are available for any individual or organization to participate in.

Investing your time in learning about and how to utilize the technology is one of the methods to make a financial investment in this organization. Currently, they are in the process of developing, which may entail learning how to design software for a certain headset, such as utilizing lumen for the magic leap one, or generating content for an upcoming platform like as clothing X.

Developing mobile applications in 2007 or generating online videos in 2006 are both examples of categories in which to invest the least amount of money. If you look about it this way, this category is equivalent to developing mobile applications in 2007. It puts you in a fantastic position to take use of those abilities as the terrain changes around you.

Chapter Six

Web 3.0

Although the term "Web 3" does not refer to a specific program, it refers to a collection of projects backed by cryptocurrency that are working together to build an ecosystem of decentralized internet services. So, what services are you referring to? There are a variety of possibilities, ranging from decentralized social media platforms rather than news managed by a single business that can suppress any views they don't like to having an open forum where individuals may openly argue and express themselves. Users may exercise control and privacy over their data when it is stored on a decentralized server. How? Blockchain technology is being utilized through the usage of cryptocurrency. It lets users not to be dependant on any single government or organization to achieve anything they desire.

To understand how web 3 works, we must first travel back in time and examine the history of web 1.0. During the dot.com era of the 1990s, websites had a function similar to that of traditional media in that they provided one-sided content that customers could consume. In a similar vein to how print newspapers charge for advertisements, websites such as Yahoo are compensated to be at the top of search results regardless of how many people click on the link.

Then, with the growth of social media, the web 2 age began, and the emphasis shifted to popular material provided by other users that was hot at the time. A number of issues occurred as a result of the blurring of the border between content consumers and producers on the web 2. Censorship and privacy concerns are the most significant of these concerns. Megatech behemoths such as Google, Facebook, and Twitter actively suppress any discussion that does not match their narrative of the world. If Donald Trump, the current president of the United States and a millionaire, can't even express himself freely on social media, what hope do you have? Web 3 changes the design of the internet to allow users not to be dependent on any single business or government so they may do anything they want.

This section will discuss some of the fundamental components of web 3 as well as some of the industry leaders in this field. These fundamental components include anything from a domain name registry to cloud data storage and computer processing, which are together referred to as smart contract platforms in the crypto-language.

The Domain Name System (DNS) - a system that manages domain names.

According to the existing system, when you go to a website, such as google.com, the bit that comes before the dot represents the subdomain, which is Google. The top-level domain is the portion of the URL that comes after the dot. The top-level domain leases the domain to the second-level domain. As a result, VeriSign, which controls top-level domains ending in dot com, rents it to Google. You will never be able to own a dot com or dot net domain name.

The difference between it and web 3 is that it is an open marketplace where people may make bids on their top-level domains. For example, the handshake is considered to be one of the most influential in this field. Their HNS token is based on a vickery-style auction, allowing anyone to purchase and rent whatever domain they like using their cryptocurrency.

Let's move on to the next component of web3, which is cloud data storage, now that we've covered the basics of what web3 is.

Cloud Data Storage is a type of data storage that is accessible from anywhere at any time. As we all know, Amazon and Google are the market leaders in cloud storage in the web 2 era. Nevertheless, in the web 3, many competitors refrain from imposing censorship or eavesdropping on their consumers. Filecoin, Siacoin, and Arweave are just a few of the cryptocurrencies that compete with Bitcoin, but there are many more. Individuals are rewarded for hosting and receiving paid in the project's native cryptocurrency, which is distributed throughout the network of peers.

Either data is kept directly on the blockchain, or the blockchain is used to keep track of payments for the individuals who are hosting the data on the blockchain. For example, with Siacoin, data is divided into groups, and hosts put up collateral to secure the network's operation. If the host fails to respond before the end of their paid hosting term, they forfeit their collateral, which serves as an incentive for them to guarantee that no data is lost. In addition, there are several duplicate hosts for each of the various groupings of hosts.

Another strategy is taken by Arweave in this case. Arweave is a blockchain that contains all of the data that has ever been. When hosts request that miners update new information, referred to as a block of information, they must demonstrate that all of the preceding information has been retained. Because it creates a permanent record, it is particularly valuable for capturing history because it allows for the preservation of information without censorship.

The third component of web 3 is computer processing, which is referred to as a Smart Contract platform in the cryptocurrency world. With web 2, information is handled on a computer or network that belongs to a single firm. However, they have the ability to modify the rules whenever they want and filter or prohibit people.

When using Web 3, information is processed on the blockchain, which makes the process totally permissionless and censorship-resistant. The code is referred to as a contract because it represents an agreement between two parties to process information stored on the blockchain. Ether, Polkadot, and Cardano are among of the pioneers in this field, as is ICP, which is a decentralized cloud platform combined with a smart contract platform, which is called internet computers.

The following are some of the most fundamental bare bones of web 3, and you may purchase all of the tokens mentioned above, as well as many more planned projects. While this is only the bare-bones architecture of how web 3 works, the possibilities for what users may accomplish with their newfound freedom of expression are virtually unlimited.

Chapter Seven

Metaverse Tech and The Health

This section will look into how humans have utilized the Metaverse to repair their bodies and modify the way their minds are wired in order to accomplish incredible feats of strength and endurance. Given that the most recent news concerning Metaverse has focused on the possibility of turning us into mindless drones, this may come as a surprise. However, while it is a possibility, I thought we could take a look at the more positive side of the multiverse instead.

We are investigating quantifiable impacts that occur to individuals in the Metaverse that have been shown by study, as well as whether or not the findings can be recreated at home or in a clinical environment. This portion of the book is 95 percent scientific, with the remaining 5 percent being my personal opinion and conjecture.

So, let us review what the Metaverse is all about. The word "Metaverse" refers to the mixing of physical and digital realms that is used to characterize the phenomenon. It includes augmented reality, mixed reality, and virtual reality. Even while the majority of people enter the Metaverse through their phones, we will eventually utilize a headgear of some form, most likely a simplified version of Oculus, Magic Leap, or Hololens.

As a builder, I spend a lot of time wearing a headset and in front of a computer, and I began to worry if this type of prolonged screen time was harmful to my health relatively early on in my career. Because I have a genotype that predisposes me to macular degeneration, I'm naturally concerned about the health of my eyes. A related question is if being engaged in these extremely detailed virtual experiences may have an effect on or influence the way my brain builds neural connections, and whether this could shrink my already limited attention span even further.

It turns out that a lot of people, particularly parents and neuroscientists, were wondering the same question, and the preliminary findings are a little startling in their conclusions. Some of the more typical bad consequences of being in the metaverse range include motion sickness, which you may already be familiar with, as well as eye strain and more serious problems such as seizures and persistent myopia or short-sightedness (which you may have heard of). The psychological consequences of spending extended amounts of time in a world where everyone is a flawless avatar are not even taken into consideration, yet there are some positive aspects to be found, and that is what this section is all about.

Although existing Virtual and Augmented reality simulations are not hyper-realistic, research has discovered that they are realistic enough that you can form brain connections after spending time in the virtual world. The process of rewiring is referred to as neuronal plasticity.

Neuroplasticity is a topic that has received much attention and is something that may be measured using brain scans. It's a skill that you'll have for the rest of your life. Your brain is constantly creating new connections between brain cells and reinforcing those that you already have and utilize on a regular basis. As a result, you should also consider cutting connections that aren't used very often.

Neuroplasticity comes into play when the brain or body is injured, which is especially true in the case of traumatic brain injury. Example: You may have injured your knee skin or suffered from a stroke that affected a portion of your brain's motor cortex that regulates your leg's movement. You may experience muscular weakness as a result of the accident, or your limb may be entirely paralyzed as well.

In order to help you regain muscular strength while you're healing, your doctor will most likely refer you to physical therapy, where you will perform exercises in a physical therapy gym. You will also need to teach your brain to generate new neurons around the damaged area if you have had a stroke in order to restore control of your limb. Anyone who has had to go through physical therapy, even for a small injury, will tell you that it is extremely difficult, dull, and may be depressing to go through.

There is an increasing body of evidence indicating that immersing someone in a virtual reality experience and then asking them to perform the same practical exercises while immersed in an immersive experience that is meaningful to them, as if they were playing a video game, is also considered physical therapy.

They have the ability to heal themselves far more quickly and effectively. Their brain will generate neurons around the injured area as a result of their VR experience, allowing them to have more movement, walk again, or regain strength. There are a handful of firms out there that are exploiting Augmented and Virtual reality to deceive your brain into jump-starting this process of neural plasticity so that it can start making new neural connections right away.

This includes a Texas-based firm called Neuro-Rehab VR Full Disclosure which is a virtual reality rehabilitation system. When I realized that this was true and backed by neuroscience, I was thrilled to have the opportunity to begin working with this small company. They have installed virtual reality physical treatment simulations in clinics and hospitals around the United States. It's incredible to witness a firm using virtual reality to improve people's lives. They are focusing on developing a virtual reality application that can be used at home. As a result, whether you require physical treatment or are healing from a sports injury, it will be quite convenient.

It is possible to use the Metaverse to improve your brain health in a variety of ways. One of my favorite firms is Helium, which has developed an immersive software to help you meditate and train your brain to remain in a meditative state for an extended period of time (and hence improve your memory).

Fundamental VR has developed an Augmented and Virtual reality program to assist surgeons in learning how to do difficult operations and procedures in the operating room. When they do a surgery for the first time, they already have muscle memory and experience under their belts. The final one I'd want to discuss is Oxford VR, which helps patients conquer anxieties and phobias in as little as two hours, which is incredible. Being able to reach the outer limits of virtual reality and neuroscience has sort of become my current interest, or at least the basis of my latest obsession, and it's a field that I'm keeping a close eye on and one in which I'd want to make a significant investment.

So what we are suggesting is the capacity for metaverse technologies like Augmented mixed and Virtual reality to modify thought patterns or attitudes and help individuals reach goals faster. It's essentially self-improvement on demand, and with neuroplasticity, goals don't have to be physical therapy or strength-related, as they are with neurorehabilitation and other forms of rehabilitation. They're also talking about assisting individuals in rewiring their brains in order to help them land a dream career, find a romantic partner, establish a business, accumulate riches, achieve financial independence, and shed some pounds. These are the kinds of things that the self-help business has made billions of dollars by attempting to market to people.

Let's take a look at what science has to say about this, because at the moment, neuroscience research indicates that this is a possibility. The new research indicates that expert meditators may concentrate on a specific condition in which they create brain waves that rearrange their neural circuitry using a mix of cognition and emotion to achieve a state of deep relaxation. There will be no instruments brought in to assist the meditators, such as a scalpel or an electrode. They're accomplishing all of this just within their own minds, which is incredible.

If you've ever heard of concepts such as the law of attraction or manifestation, this is what such practices are attempting to tap into and achieve through their use of the law of attraction and manifestation. Still, I believe they fall short of being able to do so on a consistent basis, and I believe this is due to the fact that those sorts of activities are insufficient in themselves to produce a physical or chemical change in the brain. However, if there is an option to download a $29.99 virtual reality app from the app store that does induce that emotional response and brainwave pattern that you can use once a day to tune up your thought patterns and allow you to take action in a way that will allow you to be extremely successful, you will take advantage of that opportunity.

It sounds a lot more doable than devoting ten years of one's life to becoming a masterful meditator. As a result, it is both doable and extremely thrilling. The same effect may be replicated at home by just entering a virtual reality experience of a mansion in the Hollywood Hills, which will miraculously produce the estate in real life. Technology is useful, but it isn't all that useful. There's a whole lot more to it than that.

So, going back to the beginning of the narrative, I was concerned that the Metaverse would be harmful to my health, and it appears that it might be, but it also appears that it can be beneficial to your brain if utilized properly. Due to the extent to which the Metaverse is set to take over our lives, even if it may appear to be an optional nice to have feature, I believe it is something we should advocate for to be included in the Metaverse's foundational architecture.

Chapter Eight

The Future

The globe will seem drastically different in the future as a result of several technology breakthroughs. Take, for example, the Metaverse, which would become essential to everyday existence.. It is expected that by 2040, several prominent technology businesses will make important contributions to the Metaverse, and that the Metaverse will attain universal popularity among individuals of all ages and demographics. The Metaverse and the hardware components linked with it will most likely be used by the average person in the same way that people use the internet and smartphones now.

It is possible that by 2040, the ordinary person would have a highly complex and realistic 3d avatar with several preset clothes and hundreds or thousands of distinct clothing pieces to pick from. They may have a beautifully decorated 3d living space with gateways to the metaverse worlds they have bookmarked, as well as a 3d virtual work environment with a bespoke arrangement of programs that are specifically designed to perform well in the metaverse setting.

Digital assets might be accessed using a variety of devices, including virtual reality headsets, augmented reality glasses, smartphones, smartwatches, and other similar devices, among others. These materials might be accessed through a variety of programs that were previously regarded to be unconnected in their functionality. In the Metaverse, there might be a broad range of virtual surroundings to choose from. These have a variety of applications that go beyond simple enjoyment. Fitness, education, employment and career training, product demos, virtual keynote speeches, markets for the purchase of virtual and actual objects, and other applications are examples of these use cases. Also possible is the overlaying of user-generated location-specific holograms placed over most major cities and institutions to serve as navigational aids, review tools, and 3D animations of previous events in the future.

Brain-Computer Interfaces Have the Potential to Become Commonplace.

Ray Kurzweil, a futurist and expert on emerging technologies, claimed that rika will begin linking the human neocortex to the cloud by the mid-2030s. By 2040, it's possible the prediction may come true. Brain-computer interfaces might considerably improve over the ones available in 2030, and they could be utilized for a wide range of routine tasks. They might also become regular attachments for virtual reality headsets, such as high-priced VR helmets that provide full-immersion diving experiences in virtual reality. Some brain-computer interfaces may be entirely implanted for medical applications in the near future.

When it comes to entertainment, people can utilize brain-computer interfaces to manipulate items in real-world games and virtual worlds with high acceptable precision while still having fun. Video game producers might begin using this technology into their games in the near future. For example, the power to manipulate objects with your thoughts would be extremely useful in a star wars game where you play as Jedis and Siths with force abilities, as well as in a matrix game where you play as the one, where you control the matrix.

Interfaces that seem like they belong in a bank, on the other hand, might have the most significant influence. Patients with spinal cord injuries can regain greater control over their bodies and more control over their senses when they get care from a medical professional.

Virtual assistance that is lifelike might become commonplace.

Having access to a digital virtual assistant might be a reality for everyone. Currently, language models are comparable to GPC3, but as technology advances, more powerful language models and virtual assistants will be able to be constructed on top of those language model platforms. Most websites and publications ever generated in human history might be used to train these virtual assistants, which could include text data and possibly even image data from most of those websites and publications.

They would be able to answer practically any question we posed to them, and their responses would be tailored to our specific goals, hobbies, and career aspirations. They could continually forecast what we would want to do next and provide suggestions throughout the day, rather than having us type terms into search engines every time we wanted anything. The characters might be portrayed as 3d virtual characters with which we can interact in most virtual settings, or they could take the shape of holograms when used in conjunction with augmented reality technology. These virtual characters might have intricate and distinct personalities, looks, voices, and special skills, all of which can be customized to the desired number of characters.

It is possible that autonomous vehicles will be developed.

By 2040, autonomous cars may be able to function completely without the need for human intervention. However, towns and districts that are particularly designed to enable level 5 autonomous cars would be the most important element in speeding up this progress. The city might be divided into distinct zones for autonomous cars and separate zones for people in order to lessen the likelihood of an accident occurring on any given day. It might also entail installing sensors in walls of buildings so that the location of each autonomous vehicle can be traced throughout a network of interconnected buildings. The development of these networks would allow them to track all cars, stop lights, street conditions, and other factors, forming the foundation for the world's first smart cities.

Quantum computers have the potential to become commonplace.

This might be made available to the whole population, both on a mainstream level through the cloud and on a physical level through actual devices. This development has the potential to transform the way we solve optimization issues, train and execute machine learning algorithms, and better comprehend the physical processes of nature at the subatomic level. Finance, medicine, cyber security, and material science are some of the industries that potentially profit from it.

Artificial Intelligence (AI) Has the Potential to Disrupt the Education Industry.

By 2040, artificial intelligence may be able to take over substantial portions of the educational system. Students may be able to access AI professors using virtual reality and augmented reality gadgets in the near future, according to some predictions. AI instructors might provide students with tailored instruction based on information offered to them through verbal and physical signals and hints from other students. In the case of an artificial intelligence instructor, the AI may detect what causes a student or pupil to dilate and adjust the way it teaches in order to keep the learner interested.
The use of artificial intelligence may help teachers rewrite math and English problems so that they are adapted to the basketball domain, and artificial intelligence can provide various homework assignments to each student based on their pace. In the educational system, artificial intelligence instructors will cut all of the system's fundamental expenses, allowing more individuals to access high-quality, standardized education. Pupils can be mentored and coached by human teachers in wealthier societies since they can take on fewer students.

The number of service robots in the world might reach a billion.

By the mid-2030s, the total number of service robots in the globe might reach 1 billion, with the number continuing to rise. Service robots may be broadly classified into two categories, namely personal and professional, which can be distinguished rather quickly. Personal robots come in a variety of shapes and sizes, including vacuum cleaners, lawnmowers, personal toys, mobility equipment, and pet exercise robots.

Professional service robots would be employed for business reasons and would generally be operated and overseen by employees who have undergone appropriate training and certification. Examples include medical robots, surgical procedures, firefighting robots, automated security patrols, machines to clean public spaces, delivery robots, etc. Industrial robots would also play a significant role in society, particularly in manufacturing, although they would be far less numerous than the first two sorts of robots described above. Today, most robots can instantly recognize and interact with an infinite number of objects, while also providing real-time information to their owners and users. Manufacturing employment in the United States would have been substantially eliminated as a result of the introduction of these robots. Exponentially improving machine learning, cloud computing, bandwidth, sensor technology, and other technologies might make all of this a reality.

It is possible that the first permanent lunar base will be established.

By the second half of the twenty-first century, the government and commercial companies might establish a permanent human presence on the moon. This historic achievement would be prompted in part by the projected expansion of the asteroid mining sector, which has the potential to produce billions of dollars in earnings over the next several decades. Construction of the luna foundation will be far less expensive and easier to complete with 3D printing compared with traditional approaches. On the moon's surface, rock and dust may be used to compel the creation of new tools, spare parts, and components for complete constructions. It is possible that NASA may lead the construction of this lunar facility, with assistance from the European Space Agency, the Canadian Space Agency, and a number of commercial enterprises. In addition, China and Russia may work together to develop a separate lunar outpost for themselves.

Hypersonic aircraft may soon be put into service.

It is now possible for a new generation of commercial airplanes to enter service after decades of research and development. Mach 5 is the maximum cruising speed possible for this aircraft, which is more than seven times faster than the normal passenger jet and five times the speed of sound. Hypersonic jets can travel from New York to California in 30 minutes and from New York to London in less than 4 hours, according to NASA. There are various advantages, including the fact that they can be lighter than Boeing 747s and can operate on normal runways. Furthermore, they would generate a modest amount of takeoff noise. One disadvantage is that they do not have windows since the weight of windows would be too great for this particular airplane type. It is possible that the installation of flash screen displays that show video of the outside world will provide a solution to this dilemma.

CRISPR and gene therapies have the potential to significantly reduce disease.

CRISPR, gene treatments, 3D printing, organs, blood vessels, nanoparticles, and nanorobots, among other technologies and methodologies, have the potential to reduce sickness in previously unimaginable ways. It is possible that a wide spectrum of infectious illnesses, including aids and ebola, will be treatable. Additionally, genetic factors such as sickle cell anemia and certain kinds of blindness may be treatable in the future. Thanks to gene therapy, the five-year survival rates for some types of cancer and heart disease might approach 100 percent in the near future. In the United States, the number of animals dying from cardiovascular disease might become insignificant.

Moon and asteroid mining might become a common occurrence in the future.

In commercial space enterprises, the exploitation of space resources such as metals and minerals from the moon and asteroids, which might be mined by 2040, could become the next big thing by 2040. It also has the potential to become a significant development area in terms of innovation and wealth generation in the future. Mining asteroid resources might account for only a small proportion of world commodities by 2040, according to estimates. The commodities market, on the other hand, is largely predicted to account for a significant portion of total output in the next decades. The moon and asteroid mining industries, as well as unbridled stock market speculation, have all benefited. The world's first trillionaire might be a well-known American business magnate as early as 2040, according to reports.

Carbon nanotube production might begin as early as this year.

After decades of research, it may be possible to develop a new process for the production of carbon nanotubes. Carbon nanotubes are tubes formed of carbon with sizes on the order of a few hundred nanometers. A nanotube can be made up of a single sheet of carbon atoms or it can be made up of numerous wrap layers that combine to form a hollow core. There is the potential for these constructions to stretch for thousands of kilometres in length. In addition, they have the potential to be hundreds of times stronger than steel. Carbon nanotubes have a wide range of potential applications. Bulletproof vests, water-resistant clothing, lightweight composites for autos, aircraft, and spacecraft, radiation shield materials, next-generation materials for transistors, and water purification are just a few of the technologies being developed. Some can even argue that it makes the construction of a space elevator feasible as a result of the large number.

It is possible that the first Zettascale Supercomputer will be operational.

When the Zettascale is reached in 2040, a supercomputer will be one million times more powerful than the fastest supercomputer available in the early 2020s. This system would be data-centric, which means that it would be designed to manage incredibly huge amounts of data with minimal effort. Alternatively, it may be decentralized, meaning that it would be made up of millions of smaller, less powerful components that would work together to build a collective hyper-computer that would be more powerful than any one machine.

It is possible that the Einstein Telescope will become operational.

This gravitational wave observatory, built by research institutes in the European Union, is the third generation of gravitational wave observatories. It has 10 times the sensitivity of any previous instrument, which greatly increases the distance at which black holes, collisions, neutron stars, dark matter, and other gravitational wave sources can be analyzed. The tests of Einstein's general theory of relativity would likewise be improved as a result of this. Furthermore, the previous generation of gravitational wave observatories could only study the cosmos up to a distance of 10 billion light-years from the Earth.
The einstein telescope can see much further back in time to what they dubbed the cosmic dark ages when the first stars and galaxies began to emerge.

Robots may soon be able to dominate the battlefield.

Highly mobile autonomous combat devices might be used in conjunction with a large number of frontline military people in the future. Because of their excellent machine vision, they can aim with uncanny precision and maintain superior situational awareness thanks to their strong sensors, including GPS and infrared vision, and have superior situational awareness. No human would have a chance against it if they used traditional methods of attack. These devices can be used for weeks or months at a time without the requirement for maintenance if the situation calls for it.

Space-Based Solar Energy Could Be Commercially Viable in the Future.

By 2040, it is possible that energy generated from space-based solar power will be integrated into a large number of power networks. This system entails the insertion of a number of big satellites into the Earth's orbit. Each satellite would feature a massive nanotech-based surface that could support a solar array that was over two miles in circumference. With the use of lasers, the energy emitted by the sun will be captured by these solar arrays and sent to the earth.

Large collecting dishes placed on the ground would gather the energy and turn it into useful electricity for the household. One significant advantage of this technique is that these satellites may be exposed to sunlight 24 hours a day, rather than just 12 hours a day as ground-based panels are limited to doing. Due to the possibility of space debris, high-performance shielding would be required for the panels.

In addition, some of the high-tech panels may be made of a nanotechnology-based composite that can self-heal anytime a crack or other damage occurs. It is anticipated that these sorts of satellites would arise in orbit around the moon and Mars, supplying energy to human settlements on the planets. With enough satellites orbiting Earth over the next two centuries, it is possible that practically all sunlight will ultimately be absorbed and harvested in some form or another during that time. As a result, humanity's transition to a Type 1 civilisation represents a significant stride forward. A civilisation of type 1 is capable of utilizing and storing all of the energy available on this planet.

It is likely that deep ocean mining operations will become commonplace.

It would be feasible to extract resources from the ocean floor in the future, thanks to technological advancements. Prospecting and unseat construction will be carried out by fleets of autonomous and remote-controlled robots by the year 2040, according to the International Energy Agency. The resources will be brought to the surface by hydraulic suction or continuous bucket line systems when ships or mining platforms are positioned above a potential resource deposit or deposit location.

It is anticipated that the major goal of these activities will be to obtain rare earth metals, which will be utilized as raw materials in a variety of electronic and other high-tech applications. It is possible that these resources will be of the same strategic importance as oil and natural gas in the future if there are worldwide shortages in 2040.

Methane hydrate is another viable resource, albeit it is a potentially hazardous target for deep ocean mining. It is estimated that methane hydrate represents the world's greatest natural gas reserve. Mesoporous methane hydrate deposits are made up of concentrated methane that has been trapped within frozen water crystals. To extract this energy source, the largest mining operations have already been created in Japan, China, and the United States, respectively.

Fusion energy might become commercially viable in the near future.

The International Thermonuclear Experimental Reactor (ITER), the world's biggest fusion-powered experiment, is expected to be operational by the mid-2020s. In theory, it has the potential to create a sustained output of 500 million watts, which is similar to the energy output of a conventional power plant. Its merits include being affordable and abundant in nature, as well as producing a minimum quantity of long-term radioactive waste and greenhouse gases during the course of its operation. A new experimental reactor known as spark, which might be created by MIT and a spinoff business known as Commonwealth Fusion Systems by 2040, is also being considered.

The Very Large Hadron Collider (VLHC) may soon be put into operation.

Using high-energy collisions to smash particles together, it is feasible to replicate the circumstances that existed at the beginning of the universe's history. The higher the energy, the greater the amount of time researchers can simulate and the greater the possibility of observing more novel interactions. When it comes to particle physics, the very large hadron collider will take over for the huge hadron collider, which is expected to be completed by the mid-2030s.

Its accelerated ring will be approximately 62 miles in circumference, and it will operate at a pace seven times that of the big hadron collider. In order to do this, it is necessary to significantly increase our understanding of the Higgs boson particle as well as dark matter, dark energy, and strength theory.

The development of pickle technology, which allows for the manipulation of matter at scales three orders of magnitude smaller than nanotechnology, might be aided by this new collider in the long term.

It is possible that the High Definition Space Telescope will be operational.

Thousands more Earth-like planets in our solar system's interstellar neighborhood, which is only a small fraction of our Milky Way galaxy, would be discovered by the high-definition space telescope by 2040. High-definition space telescope would be 100 times more sensitive than the Hubble Space Telescope and would be equipped with an internal coronal graph, according to the proposal. Due to the disc's ability to obscure light from a central star in the solar system, it is dark and difficult to view the planets that are more visible in that solar system.

The spacecraft will also be able to capture photographs of the planets and moons in our solar system with incredible quality and detail, according to predictions.

Chapter Nine

Primitives of Bitcoin

Many qualities of bitcoin make it a fascinating technology to deploy as well as an appealing asset to hold. Here are a few of the most notable.

Bitcoin is a pseudonymous but not anonymous network, as the name implies. This is in contrast to the present process that we must go through in order to complete a financial transaction using a credit card in the usual course of business. In the existing system, customer data such as name, address, and other personal information are associated with ordinary financial transactions. This enables surveillance capitalism to continue and expand in its current form. With Bitcoin, however, this is not the case. It is not necessary to provide personal information in order to complete a purchase.

Lastly, just to be clear, it is not fully private. Anyone has access to the full ledger, including all addresses and sums. Transactions transferring funds from one address to another may be seen by every user of the Bit- coin network. An individual can be linked to a Bitcoin address using anti-money laundering (AML) and Know Your Customer (KYC) procedures, as well as information gathered from the Internet. Companies such as Chainalysis, for example, provide this as their core service.

The Decentralized Ledger (also known as the Distributed Ledger Technology or DLT).

An open, decentralized ledger is a well-balanced design feature that allows transactions to take place in a trust-minimized environment without the need for personal information, while also allowing anybody to view the ledger and verify all account balances to ensure that reconciliation is completed. The open ledger refers to a network of decentralized nodes that are running the bitcoin software on their computers. All of the nodes have their own copy of the data that they maintain. It has a worldwide reach.

The Bitcoin blockchain network is not owned or controlled by anybody.

There are around 100,000 miners that are running the program and contributing to the security of the Bitcoin network, according to estimates.

There is no business or government that owns or controls Bitcoin, and there is no central authority. There are developers who can upgrade the program, but they can only do so after reaching agreement among three big groups of people. Bitcoin is a decentralized network in the traditional sense. When compared to centralized currencies, particularly ones that can be controlled by a central body, this is a significant benefit.

(PoW).

A proof of work is a function that is intended to be difficult to construct (expensive and time-consuming), but which can be readily validated by other people after the fact. Cryptocurrency Bitcoin makes use of the Hashcash5 proof-of-work technology. 6 This proof-of-work consensus has been reached. In Bitcoin, a mechanism is employed for block production, where the first miner that solves the proof gets to generate the new block of verified transactions and earns a mining reward (a newly minted bitcoin) in exchange for providing network security. Because it has built-in incentives for miners to compete against one another to protect the network, it is new. It also addresses the double-spend problem, which refers to the possibility of a single currency being spent more than once in a given period of time. The solution to the double-spend problem is what produces true digital scarcity, which has never been achieved until the invention of Bitcoin.

Scarcity that can be demonstrated

Prior to the invention of Bitcoin, when you transferred a digital file, you were merely sending a copy of the file. Companies made advancements in digital rights management, but doing so necessitated the creation and maintenance of those rights by a centralized authority. Until the advent of any form of third-party intermediate verification procedure, it was impossible to achieve verifiable uniqueness in the digital environment. A proven digital scarcity has been generated naturally by bitcoin, without the need for third-party verification or validation, and this is a game-changing development in the cryptocurrency industry.

There will only ever be 21 million bitcoins created in the whole history of the world. By the middle of 2020, around 18.5 million had already been mined. Due to the fact that the inflation rate of bitcoin is cut in half every four years, but the inflation rate of gold remains relatively constant or reacts to price elasticity, bitcoin is considered more rare than gold. There has never been a more difficult and rare form of money than bitcoin.

Transaction Outputs that have not been spent (UTXOs)

A unsigned transactional object (UTXO) is a concept in a certain form of blockchain. It is an output of a blockchain transaction that has not yet been spent, meaning that it can be used as an input in a new transaction on the blockchain. If there is any money left over after a transaction is completed, it will be returned to the wallet owner and may be used for future transactions by the wallet owner. UTXOs play a vital role in the operation of the ledger's accounting system, and their behavior may be studied in order to gain a better understanding of the present condition of the blockchain network. They are one of the mechanisms that enable the use of triple-entry accounting. A simple example would be if a person has three bitcoins in their wallet and spends 2.5 BTC of those bitcoin. The 2.5 BTC are transmitted to the vendor, and the remaining 0.5 BTC is the remaining unspent amount in the wallet, which is known as the UTXO.

Multisignature functionality.

Another one of Bitcoin's distinguishing characteristics as a protocol is multisignature, which refers to the necessity of more than one signature in order to approve a transaction. It enables a single Bitcoin address to delegate tasks and responsibilities to several recipients. It is possible to envision a corporate check that, for sums greater than $10,000, demands the signatures of the CEO and the CFO. Multisig also has the advantage of removing a single point of failure, which means that if one of your key signatures is compromised, you will not have all of your bitcoin stolen. Furthermore, if you had a single-signature wallet and you misplaced the keys, there isn't much you can do to restore control of the Bitcoin address associated with that wallet. There are several configuration options for the multsig feature that allow for redundancy. When it comes to Bitcoin's value increasing and establishing itself as a reserve asset, this is a vital characteristic to consider.

Digital and web-based in nature.

The fact that Bitcoin is digital contributes to the advancement of one of the six qualities of sound money. Good money must be portable, divisible, rare, acceptable, durable, and uniform in order to be effective. 7 The fact that Bitcoin is a digital currency means that it is readily transferable via the Internet, making it very portable. There are eight decimal places in it, therefore it is both divisible and uniform in this regard. Due to the fact that a bitcoin transaction may be signed and sent over a shortwave radio8, rather than over the Internet, it is likely that the term digital-based rather than Internet-based is more appropriate.

Non-Sovereign Money.

The fact that bitcoin is non-sovereign confers an extremely beneficial characteristic on it as compared to sovereign money. For the uninitiated, sovereign money refers to currency that is regulated and controlled by a government. It is true that a country's currency is safeguarded by the country's military. Nonsovereign money, on the other hand, is money that is not tied to a particular state's political structure. It is not subjected to any manipulation. Any decision made only for political reasons is nearly always a terrible decision in the long run. Bitcoin's ability to operate independently of the government is a very valuable trait. Many individuals who are aware with the issue will agree that the US dollar, which serves as the world's reserve currency at the moment, is generating tremendous problems, as explained in Part I of this book. The future international reserve currency will very certainly be a non-sovereign money system, rather than a sovereign currency.

Peer-to-Peer (P2P)

Bitcoin is a peer-to-peer payment system that does not require permission or the involvement of a third party. This is in stark contrast to the current state of affairs with regard to money. Each and every piece of money in the conventional capital system is issued by or settled through an intermediary, whether it is a central bank issuing the money or a commercial bank processing the transaction. With bitcoin, this layer is not necessary, and the associated friction (cost) and counterparty risk are eliminated. To conclude a transaction, it is also not necessary to get authorization or have faith in the other party. Ultimately, this will lower the cost of financing transactions while also allowing a greater number of individuals to benefit from this new digital financial system, which will be revolutionary. Because it is P2P and permissionless, it is more acceptable than any other form of money now in existence. Everywhere in the globe, it is transacted. By 2020, it will be available for trading in 180 different fiat currency pairs. 9 As previously stated, Bitcoin transactions do not necessitate the involvement of a trusted third party, and hence do not require authorization. This implies that neither side is required to have a bank account or to have a credit account in order to be able to make use of bitcoin.

Seizure-Resistant.

Bitcoin is a bearer asset, which implies that if you have the private keys to the asset, you have complete ownership and control over it. As a result, it is seizure-resistant. When the characteristics of being decentralized, permissionless, and secure are combined, seizure resistance is achieved. Even now, this is vital to a large number of investors. It is, without a doubt, one of the benefits of having a Swiss bank account. It is far distant and outside the jurisdiction of the United States government. Bitcoin is on the verge of becoming the Swiss bank account 2.0. If you have the private keys to an asset, you may possess millions of dollars' worth of it and move freely across international borders, certain that your assets will not be readily taken.

What Makes Bitcoin So Different?

While there are more than 5,000 different types of crypto assets, there is only one type of bit-coin. In addition to being the first, this crypto asset possesses a number of distinguishing traits that distinguish it from others. It is the asset in which an investor is seeking for a long-term investment opportunity. This has been demonstrated in a variety of ways during the past decade.

The world's first hard-capped digital currency with a predictable supply schedule

A P2P design, a hard-capped and known quantity of 21 million bitcoin, as well as a disinflationary supply schedule are all characteristics of Bitcoin, which was the first digital currency to exist. The block reward is reduced by half for every 210,000 blocks that are generated, which occurs about every four years. Because the only method for bitcoin to enter the system is through the block reward to miners, this also means that the inflation rate reduces by half as a result of the change.

Accounting with three entries is referred to as triple-entry accounting.

One of the important achievements of blockchain technology that, in my opinion, has not been sufficiently recognized is the popularization of triple-entry accounting, also known as double-entry accounting. Let's take a look at the history of accounting and ledgers to better understand why this is the case.

A ledger is a book or a set of books or collections in which accounts are kept track of. Ledgers are not a new concept. The earliest recorded usage of barcodes was more than 7,000 years ago in ancient Mesopotamia, where they were employed to monitor trade transactions and merchandise. The concept of single-entry accounting was born out of this situation. Management is straightforward — it's similar to using a checkbook. Every transaction is recorded in detail for each individual account. In order to keep track of a firm's financial state of being, inventory, and/or valuable things, every company, corporation, or organization in the world that does business must have some sort of ledger system.

After a while, single-entry accounting gave way to double-entry accounting, which basically implies that each and every transaction is recorded in two separate accounts. One account is always debited, while another account is always credited in the same transaction. Consider the following scenario: a firm owes a vendor $100, and the company wishes to pay the vendor the full amount owed. When a vendor invoice is paid, the vendor's account is credited with $100, indicating that there is no outstanding amount. The $100 is deducted from the company's cash account at the same time, indicating a reduction in available cash of $100. In double-entry accounting, the idea is that one can always see where monies are coming from and where they are going as well as the whole fiscal picture at any given moment. In 1494, Friar Luca Pacioli produced the first book on double-entry accounting, which has since become the accepted norm for almost 500 years.

As a hedge against global monetary policy, bitcoin is becoming increasingly popular. Bitcoin began to rise in value in 2020, with the price hovering at $7,200 - and there is no indication that this trend will slow down.

People are flocking to find out more about bitcoin and to determine whether now is a good moment to invest in crypto assets as a result of this upsurge in interest. However, it is critical to first grasp the precise nature of bitcoin in order to proceed. Although it isn't a stock or a typical investment, it is a currency in and of its own right. This item is classed as a commodity by the Commodity and Futures Trading Commission (CFTC) in the United States (CFTC). There will only ever be 21 million bitcoins created, and that limited quantity is one of the reasons why bitcoin is so appealing to investors.

Intriguing about Bitcoin is that it serves as a hedge or insurance policy against governments distorting and undermining the value or buying power of their own national currencies. To boost the economy during times of financial difficulty or during a cycle of deleveraging, central banks will create money to inject liquidity into the system. They do so at the cost of those who want to save money. Because bitcoin has a limited quantity, holders of bitcoin may be certain that no third party or middleman would create additional bitcoins, therefore reducing the purchase power of bitcoin. During this phase of unsound monetary policy, bitcoin serves as a store of value.

As previously noted, the pandemic is causing the national debt to grow at a faster rate than it has ever done before. The overall national debt is expected to reach between $27 trillion and $31 trillion by the end of this year, according to several forecasts. The Federal Reserve has indicated that it would continue to engage in quantitative easing indefinitely. By some estimates, there are well over $200 trillion in unfunded liabilities13, mostly in the form of Social Security and Medicare benefits, which are now being utilized in large numbers by the Baby Boomer generation. Interest rates are at their lowest point in years; equities are volatile, and political unrest in the United States and overseas is on the rise. People are becoming increasingly concerned about the state of the economy, and many are unsure where to invest their money. Many people have heard about bitcoin, but many believe it is far too dangerous, and they are unsure of how to acquire it or how its value compares to the value of other currencies or commodities, among other things. However, there are other reasons why bitcoin may be a worthwhile investment, and it can be argued that it is far more risky not to have a little amount of bitcoin in one's portfolio than it is to have a large amount.

On the Upward Spiral

In the first several days of August 2020, the S&P 500 was trading in the negative region, down around 0.3 percent. In addition to the SPDR Gold Shares ($GLD), the SPDR Total Bond Index ($BND) gained 6.9 percent, while the iShares Emerging Market Stock Index ($EEM) lost 3.0 percent and the Vanguard Real Estate Investment Trust Index ($VNQ) lost 14.3 percent. Bitcoin, on the other hand, has risen by 65.0 percent in just the first seven months of 2020. It has been steadily increasing over the previous decade, and it appears that this trend will continue. This is due to the fact that the investing community recognizes the currency's scarcity value and that it retains value in comparison to its fiat currency competitors. Because of bitcoin's hard, rare, digital, and decentralized characteristics, it is becoming increasingly desirable as more and more governments continue to issue more and more money. Increasingly, public corporations are incorporating Bitcoin into their treasury management strategies.

Cashless Economies

Many countries, such as Sweden and Israel, are attempting to reduce their reliance on currency. As central banks throughout the world continue to generate money, paper money's value diminishes at an increasing rate. Many people claim that they no longer require currency for any purpose whatsoever. It's becoming a burden, and even stores and vendors prefer to accept payments through credit card or phone. People who use bitcoin are interested in the privacy and autonomy of their money that they may obtain from a store of value – and bitcoin can supply both of these benefits. Many countries, such as India, are even phasing out their highest denominations of currency in order to combat corruption and prevent money laundering. Mr. Larry Summers, the former Treasury Secretary and director of the National Economic Council in the White House, believes it is also past time to discontinue the usage of the one hundred dollar bill. He believes that there is a correlation between high-denomination notes and crime, and that changing to cashless economies or other, safer forms of currency will be far better for investors and society as a whole. Will this contribute to the expansion of the surveillance state?

Bitcoin has experienced significant fluctuation over the years, but the gauge used to measure it has been steadily declining. As it grows more stable, bitcoin will be used in a greater number of real-world transactions, establishing it as a more credible currency that is not backed by any one government. As a result, people will be forced to rely only on technological advancement, which appears to have no difficulty gaining trust even during difficult economic times.

Chinese currency has been depreciated several times, and it is currently trading at its lowest levels versus the US dollar since March 2011.

The Chinese are also engaging in the stock market and have paused trade in their exchanges on a number of different times. Financial gurus such as George Soros believe that we are on the verge of another financial disaster on the scale of the 2008 financial crisis. These are the kinds of situations that cause investors to panic and make their holdings significantly more risky. Over time, crypto assets such as bitcoin can assist to diversify and weather dislocations in global markets, as well as to help keep money more safe, even during difficult years.

The Bitcoin Halvening Event is a one-time occurrence in which bitcoins are halved.

The Bitcoin Halvening Event is a built-in feature of the bitcoin software that regulates the supply of new bitcoins being created. Every four years, the mining reward, which is the mechanism through which freshly generated bitcoin enters the world, is reduced by half. This results in a clear and dependable money supply issuance schedule that is disinflationary since it reduces the money supply in a consistent manner over time.

The Bitcoin Halvening Event has occurred three times in the history of the cryptocurrency.

First, in 2012, then in 2016, and finally, in 2020. The first was held in 2012. For the first two events, there was a highly bullish period for bitcoin from one to nine months following the event, with bitcoin growing in value at various points during each of those periods. We'll have to wait until 2021 to see how the third event plays out, although at the time of writing this book, the majority of investors were quite positive on the Halvening Event's prospects. An analysis released in 2020, which took a pricing model used for precious metals and adapted it to bitcoin, contributed to some of the excitement. Anyone who understood anything about bitcoin in 2020 was almost certainly familiar with the stock-to-flow paradigm.

Other Methods of Determining the Value of Bitcoin

When speaking with anyone who is interested in bitcoin trading, the question of "How much is bitcoin worth?" is often posed at some point. It's a difficult question to respond to. Here are three factors to take into consideration when determining how much bitcoin is worth.

As a financial asset or commodity

For those who wish to try their hand at estimating the value of bitcoin in the context of a commodity, one approach may be to estimate its worth as a percentage of the overall value of gold. The total market capitalization of all gold presently mined today is around $10 trillion. Because gold is a non-consumable commodity that is primarily utilized as a store of value, it is an excellent commodity for use as a comparison. Every aspect of life is going into the digital realm, and bitcoin may prove to be a valuable asset for future generations. Even if bitcoin were to capture just ten percent of the total value of gold, the market capitalization of bitcoin might reach $1 trillion. Bitcoin has a market capitalization of more than $200 billion as of today.

Tom Lee, co-founder of FundStrat Global Advisor, is attempting to value bitcoin in this manner, however he only uses 5 percent of the value of gold. The value of bitcoin would remain at $500 billion, but I believe it is considerably higher than that when you consider how many asset classes are now utilized as a store of value, where the affluent lodge their money for the long term, including gold and silver. According to some estimates, 30 percent of all real estate sales in prominent places such as Los Angeles and New York are for properties that will not be used and are instead acquired as a long-term store of wealth. Furthermore, how much beautiful art is acquired, put in vaults where it will never be viewed again, and gathered simply for the purpose of accumulating wealth?

He also discusses the network effect (its acceptability) and Metcalfe's Law in his capacity as a Technology/Network expert. The following is how value is established: the greater the level of interaction, the greater the amount of value generated. Because of the network effect, the value of bitcoin will rise as the number of individuals who use it continues to grow. This concentration on bitcoin as a technology or as a social network demonstrates the significant potential for nonlinear growth.

Chapter Ten

The Blockchain

They say that necessity is the mother of all inventions, and this is true. After the 2008 financial crisis, Bitcoin, the world's first deployment of blockchain technology, came into being. To suggest that there was a crisis was an understatement, given the situation of the markets, the enormous deflation, and the uncertainty that pervaded the financial markets at the time. It was necessary to find a solution that incorporated a distinct way of thinking in order to provide future choices.

Bitcoin, which is currently in the spotlight and is the most well-known of all cryptocurrencies, is the solution to this problem. Blockchain technology, one of the most significant technological breakthroughs of our generation, is the foundation upon which bitcoin (and all other crypto assets) is built. It's critical to grasp the fundamentals of crypto assets before you can properly understand them themselves.

Over the past several years, the term "blockchain" has been more and more prevalent in everyday conversation. It's being used in Uber rides and dinner parties, board rooms and classrooms, playgrounds and town halls, and it's swiftly becoming the word of the generation. Despite the fact that it is regularly utilized, there are many people who do not fully comprehend what it is, how it works, or why it is so important.

What Exactly Is Blockchain Technology?

Let's start with a straightforward illustration. A blockchain is a collection of blocks that have been connected together. Simple! "Blocks of what?" one would wonder in response to this. We'll have to get a bit deeper into this now. According to Dictionary.com, "a blockchain is a sort of decentralized database system that is built on connecting together prior entries in safe blocks of information," which means "a chain of information." 1 The following line is an excellent example of something that actually doesn't mean anything, so let's break it down to make sense.

"Decentralized" is the first and most crucial term to remember in this context. In other words, there is no one (centralized) governing body. Because most things in the world are centralized, it's difficult to see this happening. A centralization of power exists in all aspects of life: government; enterprises; organizations; non-profits; even families. Generally speaking, each of these creations is overseen by a person (or group of people), and the entities themselves are frequently in control of other entities. With this governance system, which ensures that there is always someone "at the top" or "in control," we're at ease. It appears like people and enterprises all across the world are working independently, but this is actually done at the pleasure of a central authority in almost every case.

Let's continue to dissect our definition, which states that it is a decentralized database system in the next sentence. We already know that databases store information, therefore we can conclude that a decentralized database stores information in several locations rather than in a single central one. Interesting about this is that each place does not only have a portion of the data; each site has all of it. There is a duplicate of all of the data in each place. This is critical, and we'll get to the reason why a little later.

After that, we get to the conclusion of our definition, which is based on connecting previous data in safe blocks of information. Blockchain is comprised of "blocks and chains," as the phrase goes. It appears to be more scary than it actually is. It essentially implies that as new information becomes available, it is attached to the information that came before it. Consider the concept of data being piled on top of data that is stacked on top of data.

One way to think about this is as a stack of papers (blockchain). Each sheet of paper in the stack contains a piece of information (transaction). It is our practice to write down any new knowledge as soon as it comes to us (block). The information on the sheet of paper is accumulated over time as we continue to work on it (block interval). Once the paper is completely filled, we produce copies and distribute them to everyone in the network. Every duplicate is stacked on top of the stack of paper that came before it in the process of being created. Information written on paper is irreversible (immutable) after it has been published - because each peer in the network receives a copy, everyone is aware of the content and sequence of the data. Everybody can see and agree on the permanent recording system, and it is immutable once it is in place. In this example, each piece of paper represents a block, and each block is added to the top of the stack, creating a chain that is always expanding — the blockchain. Easy!

This is extremely difficult to do, which is why blockchain technology is considered a breakthrough in and of itself. We did not have the capacity to have a group of peers working together in a way that maintained integrity and transparency prior to the invention of the blockchain. We were unable to establish decentralized entities that operated under a single governance structure.

Blockchain Characteristics

There are several individual components that enable this technology to function, so let's take a closer look at the characteristics and parts that enable blockchain protocols to function.

Immutable

Blockchains are immutable — that is, they cannot be changed – which is a feature that is both valuable and unusual. Virtually every other technology now in use, including financial instruments, has the capability of altering transactions. They have the ability to be overwritten. Financial data can contain bank balances and credit card activities as well as scores and scores of loans and transactions and many other things. Almost everything in the general transactional world is susceptible to manipulation, from delivery to orders to health information to financial records. This is due in no little part to the fact that the vast majority of data is under the control of a single organization.

Blockchains, on the other hand, do not operate in this manner. Once a transaction is recorded into a block on a blockchain, it is permanently stored there and cannot be modified by anybody else in the network. Period. As a result, if Bob transfers Sally one bitcoin (BTC), Sally will have one bitcoin. That particular deal is unassailable. We learnt previously that it is written on the blockchain and that all participants in the network validate it, resulting in everyone having a copy of the transaction. The transaction on the chain could be found if Bob claims it didn't happen, and even if Bob took Sally to court (that BTC may be worth $1 million someday!), we could find it and know the truth. It can't be argued with. Now, this does not imply that Sally will always be in possession of that one Bitcoin. She may choose to spend some of it, but it is a very different trans-action from the one described here. Anyone who claims that Bob did not give Sally one bitcoin will be proven wrong in the long run. The fact that this level of assurance occurs in just a few places on the planet is very significant, not only in the context of currency transactions but also in the context of transactions of any sort.

Transparent

Blockchains are all transparent, which is a basic aspect of the technology. This implies that everyone is aware of what everyone else is doing – and has been doing – throughout the duration of time. There is no obscurity or ambiguity in this case. There are a few blockchains that are dedicated to privacy, but they are few and far between. Every node in the network (every miner) possesses a copy of each and every transaction that has ever taken place on the network, which gives blockchains their distinctive transparency. If there is ever a doubt regarding the information included in a specific block, all that has to be done is to check the information contained in the block by other nodes (miners) in the blockchain. If there is ever a disagreement, all of the nodes in the network may be verified to see who is correct. Transparency is critical since it is what motivates everyone to "play by the rules" in the first place.

Permissionless

Permissionless is just a slang term for "public," and as such, a permissionless blockchain is a public blockchain that does not need the creation of an account or the acquisition of permission to use. Public blockchains are analogous to other forms of public infrastructure, such as the Internet. Everyone, regardless of their affiliation, is permitted to engage in block-chain transactions without prior clearance. Unlike a permissioned blockchain, which, as you have no doubt deduced by now, refers to a private blockchain, a permissioned blockchain is a public blockchain.

There are certain parallels between the two types of blockchains.

In order to establish the viability and finality of transactions, they employ consensus methods, which are immutable and distributed ledgers. Permissioned blockchains, on the other hand, are required to have the consent of a central or governing entity by their very nature. If I have done my job so far, you are no likely thinking to yourself, "Wait a minute! "The whole goal is to avoid having a centralized authority," you may say, and you would be accurate. As Satoshi Nakamoto envisioned, a permissionless blockchain is the purest version of the technology. It allows everyone to participate in the system because there is no single person in authority. Blockchains such as Bitcoin and Ethereum operate without the need for authorization. Anyone is welcome to take part. Anyone has the potential to become a miner (though it is certainly more expensive to do now than it was 10 years ago). There is no centralized administration.

IBM's Hyperledger Fabric, on the other hand, is a permissioned block-chain technology. It has an access control layer that gives or revokes user permissions based on the user's behavior. Some circumstances may benefit from this, while others may not. In the case of a business, for example, not every decision about corporate transactions should be made public. Furthermore, because permissioned block chains have a smaller, more regulated footprint by nature, the speed with which they may be implemented is typically higher, and adjustments and management are generally simpler when there is no need to reach agreement. Using permissioned blockchains, on the other hand, has the disadvantage of putting us in a state of single point of failure and dependent on a private and centralized entity.

Cryptocurrencies should almost always be permissionless and administered on public blockchains in order to properly realize their full potential in broad use, according to the crypto community.

Chapter Eleven

Themes of Investing

Self-Sovereign Money that is sound

One investing topic is to make investments in decentralized money that is digital, rare, hard, nonpolitical, and no sovereign. One of the most compelling arguments in favor of investing in cryptocurrency, primarily bitcoin, is the desire to have an insurance policy against the manipulation of the money supply by central banks throughout the world. This is a hedge against the greatest monetary experiment in history, which began with quantitative easing as a response to the 2008 financial crisis but has evolved and grown in scope since then. Central banks all across the world have cut interest rates to zero percent or even negative rates in order to stimulate the economy. They've all maintained or increased the size of their balance sheets. There seemed to be no end in sight.

As a Protective Measure

Japan's central bank, the Bank of Japan (BoJ), will hold more than 80 percent of all Japanese equities exchange-traded funds (ETFs) by 2020.

The phrase "Lost Decade" was used to describe to Japan's economic stagflation (disinflation) crisis that lasted for a decade in the 1990s. The phrase "financial crisis" was first used in 2001, and the continuous crisis has now lasted over three decades. It takes decades for a deflationary cycle to come to an end, and that is the problem with it. It comes to an end when the central bank buys back all of the bonds, causing the currency to collapse.

Venezuela is located at the other extreme of the spectrum. Inflation in the country reached 9,586 percent in the year 2019. That's a lot of money. The currency was debased to the point where it was no longer valuable, and the currency collapsed.

In any case, it is the government's interference that is to blame for both of these consequences. It is necessary to separate money from the state. The best we can do in the absence of political will to achieve this aim is to purchase insurance or a hedge against fiat-denominated assets, which include currency, debt, and stock market investments. Gold and bitcoin serve as a hedge against inflation. Both are extremely liquid and do not involve any counterparty risk. Bitcoin, as previously outlined, possesses a number of characteristics that distinguish it as a superior hedge against sovereign-based fiat money. Foreign currency that is not tied to a single government will be vital in the future because it eliminates any political risk connected with a certain country, which will be critical in the next generation of global reserve assets.

The International Monetary Fund (IMF) Backdrop

The implementation of increasingly novel types of monetary intervention by central banks throughout the world, as we've explored throughout the book, is on the rise. Interest rates have been set at zero percent all throughout the world, and in certain situations, negative interest rates have been established. Central banks are now experimenting with a variety of different types of balance sheet growth. Japan's central bank, the Bank of Japan (BoJ), is in the midst of the most significant phase of the country's balance sheet growth. It purchases Japanese corporate debt as well as Japanese stocks through the purchase of exchange-traded funds (ETFs). The European Central Bank, like other central banks, has held several conversations regarding purchasing stocks. The previous Federal Reserve chair Janet Yellen has also stated that the Federal Reserve does not need to purchase stocks at this time, but that Congress should rethink authorizing it. The coronavirus did nothing but expedite the activities of global central banks. As a result of the rapid spread of the pandemic beginning in March 2020, the Federal Reserve initiated a $700 billion quantitative easing program. Because the economy was effectively shut down, the stock market fell into freefall. The Fed then launched a second attempt that was worth $1.5 trillion — the largest possible balance sheet expansion at the time, which served as their bazooka moment. However, the government's $2 trillion fiscal stimulus measure was approved in an effort to assist residents, small companies, and corporations in dealing with the epidemic, but it was only the beginning of their efforts. The Fed then promised "QE to infinity," which culminated on April 9 with the declaration of another $2.3 trillion in balance sheet growth, as well as the announcement that they could and would purchase corporate bonds, something that had never been done before in the United States. All of this monetary and fiscal stimulation will have an effect on inflation and the value of the US dollar in the future. Bitcoin, with a maximum supply of 21 million bitcoins and exceptional money qualities, is an excellent investment instrument for those seeking a safe haven for their money.

A Digital Reserve Asset is a type of digital reserve asset.

Bitcoin is also a reserve asset in the new digital financial network, which is powered by blockchain technology. It is the digital asset that serves as a store of value for the cryptocurrency. So it makes for an excellent digital candidate for serving as a reserve asset upon which additional digital assets might be built. The book The Bitcoin Standard argues in favor of this position. The establishment of a digital financial system based on sound money is a fundamental principle of the Bitcoin revolution.

Asset That Is Surveillance-Resistant

A element of the sound money investment theory is that we need to create our portfolios on top of assets that are resistant to monitoring. We are presented with an option between two realities. Do we give governments the authority to monitor and control every effort and activity, as they do in China? Is it OK for us to give companies access to all of our data and to allow them to monitor our actions on a continuous basis through our mobile phones, as is the case in the United States? One of the goals of the crypto movement is to maintain some level of individual anonymity. This sound money investing concept is based on the realization of this demand.

Asset with Seizure-Resistant Properties

Finally, the sound money investment thesis includes the notion of a seizure-resistant asset into its analysis of the financial markets. Given that bitcoin does not require the participation of a third party in order to complete a financial transaction, it also eliminates the potential of a third party to tamper with or intervene in a financial transaction. The principle of immutability is incorporated into the bitcoin system from the beginning. Bitcoin, when combined with cryptography and the usage of keys, creates a permissionless, seizure-resistant asset that is difficult to counterfeit. As a result, the sound money thesis predicts that the market will place a high premium on this attribute. Finance that is decentralized or open

After the initial coin offering (ICO) boom, decentralized finance (also known as open finance) became the most talked-about topic in the crypto world. Within a year, we observed a jump from $0 to over $1 billion in collateral commitments into the open finance system, which will continue through 2019 and into 2020. The desire has shown itself. What makes open finance so effective is that it operates without the need for authorization and without the involvement of a third party that can be relied on.

You don't need to create an account, and you don't require anyone's permission to do so. DeFi is based on a public blockchain, which means that anybody with an Internet connection may access and use it. Two things are made possible as a result of this. As for the demand side, it provides an opportunity for investors to generate new types of cash. Investors may supply collateral into the system using smart contracts, and the system can generate a new kind of stable currency known as stablecoins, all in the name of sound money policy. This is a new type of decentralized money that is backed by other digital assets such as bitcoin. As for investors, they can use the freshly generated digital money to fund the initial creation of capital, which is debt in the form of lending, on the demand side. This results in the creation of an interest rate for the currency. It is responsible for the creation of banking services. The same investors, as well as other investors, might then use the borrowed money to make other investments. This is the fundamental building block of a financial system.

Banking the Unbanked

Open finance aspires to deliver a new digital and permissionless version of traditional financial services that may be accessed by anybody, anywhere in the world. As of this writing, only around 1.5 billion individuals in the globe have access to checking accounts, much alone financial services in general. Achieving the goal of providing financial services to all 4.5 billion people, while simultaneously lowering the friction of cost and time for current customers, would generate significant economic activity. All of those 4.5 billion individuals might have access to accounts for making money transfers, saving money, and borrowing money if they wanted to.

Digital Currency/Stablecoins.

However, this is about much more than simply banking the unbanked. Consider the individual in Africa who has never had access to the financial markets before. When a family is able to borrow against an asset such as land, this is often when the family's initial capital formation occurs. The majority of people who have risen out of poverty have done so by taking out a loan against their property in order to raise funds in order to start a business that generates income. That person in Africa, on the other hand, never had a clear title to his property, couldn't show he owned it, and as a result, was unable to borrow against it. He was never given the opportunity to establish a business and generate income for himself. Even if he had begun with a tiny investment. The open finance system allows anybody, regardless of their starting point (one satoshi, the smallest unit of bitcoin), to get a collateralized loan on some digital asset and borrow against that asset. Following that, they may put the borrowed money to work, generating greater economic value than the loan interest amount and generating cashflow as a result. Equity is the amount of cashflow that has been saved. With money, debt, and equity, you've created a whole financial system that doesn't require any permission or involvement from a third party. What kind of force might be released on a global scale if it happened?

Lending

As a result of the creation of digital money by a decentralized bank, an increasing number of participants are able to lend. To yet, only collateral lending has taken place through the tying up of digital assets in smart contracts and the loan of money at a rate of interest. Borrowers receive particular interest rates, lenders receive certain interest rates, and the spread is paid to the whole system that links borrowers and lenders. Essentially, this is how traditional banking operates, and it has now been reproduced in DeFi. Smart contracts are used to deliver all of DeFi's loan services, which are available on the DeFi platform. They allow for collateralized loans to be made in a permissionless environment, which is made possible by the use of public blockchains. At the moment, Ethereum is the clear victor in the race to build a Layer 1 blockchain that can supply DeFi services.

Derivatives

Speculators and investors will want derivatives in order to hedge their holdings or speculate on the market. There are various decentralized autonomous organizations (DAOs), or corporations, that are provided by DeFi that provide digital derivatives contracts that are often enforced by smart contracts. Companies, or decentralized autonomous organizations (DAOs), such as Synthetix, FTX, Augur, and others, supply derivatives in the DeFi area.

Insurance

Decentralized insurance began in 2020 with the formation of a mutual insurance business, similar to those found in traditional markets. Nexus Mutual and Opyn are two insurance companies that provide coverage for a variety of services and assets. Providing protection, hedging, or speculating services in an unrestricted, decentralized manner creates a value proposition for the user. Additionally, faster payments and greater flexibility are provided to its members as a result of this. This enables anybody to create revenue by establishing themselves as an insurance firm or person and accepting specific structured risks in exchange for a premium. DeFi insurance also covers technological and financial risks that are not covered by any other insurance firms, and when combined with other services, may be used to create more complicated financial products than are now available. If an investor wishes to cover the risk associated with the use of a smart contract, the risk associated with a loan, or other financial hazards, they may do so through the use of DeFi insurance services. Now that investors can hedge and protect against risk, the use of these services will become more sophisticated, and more investors will flock to DeFi as a result.

Decentralized Exchanges (DEXs)

Investors will no longer need to log onto an exchange and place market or limit orders in order to purchase or sell their digital assets in the future. It will be carried out inside a larger framework that includes a user interface (UI) with well defined goals and regulations, and it will be governed by smart contract technology. Additional- ly, investors will be aiming to put together more sophisticated transactions that incorporate several asset classes as well as lending and borrowing as well as insurance and transfers, as well as the buying and selling of derivatives. These more complicated transactions will be sought after by investors since they reduce risk, boost return, and improve total risk-adjusted returns for the investor. In truth, insurance is a critical component of an investment strategy that the ordinary investor fails to consider because he or she is unaware of it, does not have access to it, or believes it is prohibitively expensive. A further innovation is the incorporation of pro-grammatic money, which is set to revolutionize the way in which money is kept, processed, and transferred as units representing stores of value. DEXs, or decentral-ized exchanges, will fundamentally alter the way we invest and the way the entire process is carried out in the future.

The Autonomy Era Has Arrived

The Age of Autonomy is a long-term investing thesis that is based on the concept of autonomy. Crypto assets that an investor may choose to include in this investing thesis will alter over time, depending on the investor's preferences. Platform crypto assets will play a significant role in the early stages of this investing thesis, since there is a race to determine which blockchains will be deployed in which contexts. In the DeFi space, Ethereum has established itself, but there are still other sectors where it might make a difference. Investing in public infrastructure that will encourage autonomy and autonomous operations is the central element of the strategy.

Increasing the amount of public infrastructure that is created will take time. DeFi is a vital component in enabling investors and operators to connect with services that provide hedging, insurance, trading, lending, and other financial services through the use of autonomous contracts. The next step of the Age of Autonomy investment thesis involves tying all of these services together in order to provide autonomous execution capabilities. Following that, the development of market-places for real-time interaction will be carried out through the execution of autonomous contracts. It is most probable that such markets would function as decentralized exchanges (DEXs), where smart contracts will be used to shift assets and money programmatically, rather than through a human computer user interface. Another part is the administration of these crypto assets, as well as the self-organization of humans in various decentralized autonomous organizations (DAOs) and decentralized autonomous communities (DACs) to organize and synthesize information into objectives and actions. All of these concepts and devices have an important role to play in the Age of Autonomy.

Conclusion

Now that you are aware with what the metaverse is and how you might invest in it, it is prudent for you to apply the new information you have gained from the contents of this book in a practical manner. You should be prepared to make investments in equities, NFTs, virtual world tokens, and other financial instruments. Even before the advent of NFTs, websites such as Decentraland and The Sandbox made it possible for anyone to purchase virtual pieces of land and even construct their own settings using the technology. The metaverse is becoming a reality, and as we get closer to that reality, we should expect to see more investment possibilities emerge in this arena.

CPSIA information can be obtained
at www.ICGtesting.com
Printed in the USA
LVHW060403150422
716000LV00012B/219